TABOR R. STONE is an architectural consultant for the Office of the United States Air Force Surgeon General.

TABOR R. STONE

BEYOND
THE *AUTOMOBILE*

Reshaping
the
Transportation Environment

A SPECTRUM BOOK

Prentice-Hall, Inc.
Englewood Cliffs, N.J.

Cartoons on p. xii reprinted by permission of Virgil Partch and the United States Steel Corporation.

HE
151
S745 / 21,558

Current printing (last number): 10 9 8 7 6 5 4 3 2 1

C-13-076026-9
P-13-076018-8

Library of Congress Catalog Card Number 72-140266

Printed in the United States of America

Prentice-Hall International, Inc. (*London*)
Prentice-Hall of Australia, Pty. Ltd. (*Sydney*)
Prentice-Hall of Canada (*Toronto*)
Prentice-Hall of India Private Limited (*New Delhi*)
Prentice-Hall of Japan, Inc. (*Tokyo*)

To Laila, Tom, David, Monica, Stanley, Bart, and Kristine

CONTENTS

PREFACE

PROJECTIONS BASED on our current population-growth trends indicate that the 1970 United States population of 200.3 million will boom to 266.2 million by the year 2000, an addition of over half a million new people within a thirty-year period. While the growth rate in this country is slow compared to many others, it is perhaps more significant, as each American baby demands approximately fifty times as much from the life-support systems of the planet as, for example, the average baby in India.[1]

Our population growth is placing great stresses on our facilities and service systems, and such stresses are growing by leaps and bounds. This is a book about one of these service systems—transportation. It examines our present methods of handling transportation and suggests an alternate approach based on the conclusion that our conventional methods cannot meet the demands of our growing population, and that attempting to meet these demands by these methods will, in the long run, prove more harmful than beneficial.

At the time of this writing, the American Association of State Highway Officials is petitioning Congress for a highway construction package of $320 billion, to be spent between now and 1985 for the expansion of our urban and regional roadway systems, primarily through the construction of urban expressways.[2] Highway proponents see the continuous expansion of the roadway system as the answer to our growing transportation demands. They regard the detrimental effects of constructing expressways in the urban and semiurban landscape as a necessary evil, to be glossed over as "redevelopment."

But the residents of such "redeveloped" areas see it differently: the

1. *U.S. News & World Report,* March 2, 1970, p. 37.
2. Ibid., p. 35.

ix

Federal Highway Administration has announced that construction of 128.4 miles of urban highways in sixteen cities has been held up by organized local resistance based on opposition to noise and pollution, destruction of homes, and defacement of historic developments, as well as resultant shifts in property values.[3]

This book explores the notion that a very large scale commitment to rail and bus transit systems, rather than the perpetuation and expansion of the automobile/roadway system, might prove more appropriate in long-range sociological and environmental terms, as well as in functional terms. This is a generalized discussion, as the scope of the topic demands simplification of many complex issues. It is not intended to be the definitive work on transportation; it is instead the outline of a proposal. Placing this proposal in the context of historical developments in order to demonstrate the rationale behind it has necessitated a survey of past and present transportation practices and effects—a survey that concentrates on the land use effects of transportation-system layouts and neglects other elements of the transportation scene, such as the cost and speed discussions associated with transportation economics.

In fact, cost and speed factors may prove to be secondary to other concerns when contrasted with the alternatives. An expensive rail system might prove cheaper in the long run than a supposedly less-expensive highway system when we consider the urban-blighting effects of the latter. And speed discussions become irrelevant in the face of congestion problems during commuter hours, problems that threaten the entire automobile/highway system and are not paralleled within the high-passenger capacity railed systems.

The obvious risk of basing a book on a proposal is that the proposal tends to take on the aspects of a panacea—a step-by-step solution to the world's problems—as it tends to be argued outside the context of the overall situation. Sociologist and planner Herbert Gans cautions that most physical planners make this mistake in that their basic assumption that the physical environment plays a very influential role in man's social environment is not conclusive, and that physical planning is currently of a lower priority than resolving the problems caused by poverty and segregation.[4] On the other hand, we face the urgent problem of meeting population pressures on our physical facilities and systems. This book is written in the conviction that we cannot properly meet these pressures in a conventional manner, and to continue to attempt to do so will develop a greater negative influence on the physical and social environment than we can tolerate.

3. Ibid.
4. *Psychology Today*, March 1970, p. 58.

A full listing of those to whom I am indebted for moral support and technical assistance in the production of this text is not possible here; however, the following have made the most significant contributions and deserve acknowledgment: Don Evans, Coy Howard, Kay Howard, Jim Johnson, Girard Kinney, Phil Tobey, Phil Will, Karen Will, Glen Willis, and my wonderful wife, Laila. A special word of thanks goes to Mrs. Dorothy Troha, whose words of encouragement to this neophyte were instrumental in starting the project rolling.

"Do you realize, sir, that if your invention should gain popular acceptance—which I do not for one moment believe it will—we should have to provide paved roads, throughout the length and breadth of the country, thousands of pumping stations to supply ready access to fuel, and innumerable vacant lots in every city in which to park the vehicles? Take my advice and forget this folly, Henry."

"The whole business is economically unsound, gentlemen. With a train of this length and forty miles of track, we find that only .0568 per cent of the track will be in use at any given time, representing a constant idle investment of 99.9432 per cent."

One

THE CHALLENGE

"The growth of megalopolis owes much to the automobile,
but highway traffic jams are beginning to strangle city
activities and to take the pleasure and efficiency out of driving
a car. At the same time, cars contribute to the ruination
of other means of transportation, made more necessary
than ever by the massive tidal currents of people and
goods. . . . The highways and the automobiles have been
a great help in alleviating for a time the flow of traffic
through the crowding of megalopolis. Now, however, a
degree of saturation has been reached that calls for
new solutions."

—Jean Gottman[1]

- In 1963 a massive traffic jam paralyzed the center of Boston for over five hours.
- In 1965 the New Jersey Turnpike was the scene of a forty-five-mile-long jam of 1.5 million automobiles which lasted for over seven hours.

1. As quoted in Claiborne Pell, *Megalopolis Unbound* (New York: Frederick A. Praeger, Inc., 1967), p. 57.

- In 1970 automobile-produced air pollution choked Eastern cities at record-setting hazard levels.
- Every day at least 9,000 people are injured or killed on our streets and highways.
- Every day expressway construction robs people of their homes, destroys their neighborhoods, and blights the countryside and cities alike.

WE ARE FACING a transportation crisis, one that becomes more critical as time goes on, a crisis which threatens to overwhelm us while we are standing around seeking solutions. Concurrently, we are facing a land-usage crisis as we face the task of accommodating an additional half-million people by the year 2000 in a landscape that has been shaped more to fit the needs of the automobile than to fit the needs of man.

We need to develop comprehensive planning policies involving all the aspects of both transportation planning and land-use planning. Transportation determines much more about the nature of the physical environment than we commonly recognize—in fact, transportation acts as the most effective single form-determining element of the man-made environment, and deserves our immediate attention as such.

We can argue that the realignment of any single environmental element would have little significant effect on the total scene . . . that all factors, such as population distributions, economic structures, land-use policies, and public attitudes, as well as transportation policies, must be changed concurrently if we are to produce any significant environmental changes at all.

Unquestionably, any effort to produce a planned change in our environmental evolutionary patterns (such as will be necessary to accommodate our great population growth properly) must be an across-the-board one. We cannot simply extract a single environmental element, change it, and expect that change to produce both dramatic and desirable results throughout the spectrum of environmental facilities. On the other hand, we cannot make changes with most of the elements of that spectrum while neglecting a specific major element and expect any significant success in terms of comprehensive environmental planning.

I believe that we are now following this latter course by concentrating our planning efforts only in the area of urban economics, housing, land-use controls, urban "renewal," new-towns, and other such elements of the environment. I maintain that we are neglecting a key element—transportation—and are failing to recognize its environment-shaping implications and its potentials. Ironically, we are neglecting (in terms of planner-based control) a transportation system that has been built up by industry, certain governmental agencies, and an enthusiastic public into the most extensive and elaborate in the world, one that is undeniably a dominant factor in the urban environment.

Transportation must be discussed on a dual level: that of its functional role and that of its environmental role. Our present transportation techniques are failing to serve us properly in both areas. I believe that this is basically due to an inappropriate application of transportation system types to the motion tasks involved, and also because comprehensive control over both the functional and environmental aspects of transportation does not exist.

Some communications analysts see advanced communications devices eliminating the need for the great commuter movements we struggle with at this time . . . however, the gadgetry has yet to arrive . . . and if it does, it will most likely have the effect the telephone did: instead of cutting down on the overall motion patterns, this device simply expanded the scope of man's activities. Also, we hear the argument that we are gaining more leisure time as the country becomes more affluent, which suggests that noncommuter movements are becoming a greater part of the total movement scene. Unhappily, this is but a myth, as the average American work-week has actually increased from 40.6 hours in 1941 to 41.1 hours (and rising) in 1965.[2] The suburban population of 54.5 million in 1960 has grown in ten years to 69.6 million: suburban/urban commuter movements are very much with us, and demand much more from us than wishful thinking.

The transportation problem is not beyond resolution. However, at this point in time, solutions will not come cheap. Our best course, for reasons outlined in the following chapters, is to make a vast investment in railed transit systems, on a scale never attempted before, in order to serve us properly, as both a passenger and a resident of the environment.

I limit discussion to the movement of people, as I believe that this is the critical element of the transportation situation. I do not wish to imply by this that freight movement is not an important element, or that it is to be neglected in the process of developing comprehensive planning policies. In fact, serving the movement needs of people in an area basically solves the freight movement needs for that same area, as most goods (retail merchandise, foodstuffs, equipment, supplies, etc.) are used or exchanged within the same activity centers where the people work. As is true now, the transportation system that carries people at certain times of the day will be able to move goods during the "off" hours.

In order to recognize, in the hopes of realizing, the potential benefits of better aligning our transportation methods with functional and environmental goals, we must explore the operational characteristics of the system types available to us, in

2. Economic Report of the President, 1966.

terms of their relationships to these goals. The following chapters outline the two basic system types, discuss their operational and environment-affecting characteristics, and demonstrate what I believe to be a more valid application of these types to our needs.

Figure 1-1.
Photo by author.

Two

RANDOM-ROUTE AND FIXED-ROUTE SYSTEMS

A MEANINGFUL DISCUSSION of urban transportation is not possible without first establishing a common understanding about the nature of transportation technology. In this study, specific transportation gadgetry is not too pertinent, as continual research and development, especially in railed systems, makes quickly obsolete any compilation of a catalogue of such devices.

What is pertinent, however, is the recognition that conventional and new transportation developments can be classified into two basic system types. The first is characterized by the automobile/roadway system, and the second by the train/railway system.

The conventional automobile/roadway system is a transportation system with a vast network of roadways (streets, highways, expressways) and a vehicle which acts as a free agent on this network, in the sense that the vehicle, at most times, has a great number of route options. I call this transportation category the random-route system. The random-route system is one composed of a great network of pathways, with the vehicle unattached to the pathways (meaning not hooked to the pathway by rails or electronic guidance devices), and capable of following any desired route on the path network, while having the option of changing routing at any point along the way.

The random-route system is the dominant transportation system in the United States today, and it is one with which we are all quite familiar.

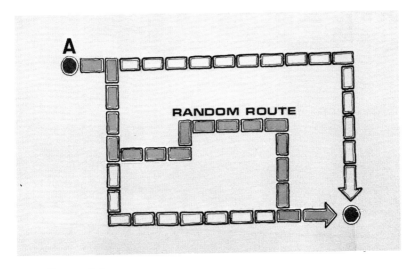

Figure 2-1.
The random-route system. Drawing by Don Evans.

Conversely, the train/railway system comprises a type almost opposite in nature to the random-route system. This category, which I call the fixed-route system, involves a limited (relatively) number of roadways, with the routes of the vehicles being predetermined. Most commonly, the fixed-route vehicle is physically attached to its roadbed, as with the conventional railroad train, although this is not essential. The most common form of urban transit, the city bus, operates on the random-route street system, but the city bus falls into the category of being a fixed-route system, since it must stick to pre-planned routes in its daily movements, and must stop at pre-planned points within certain time limits during the day.

Fixed-route systems can be classified into short-range, medium-range, and long-range subcategories. The most inter-

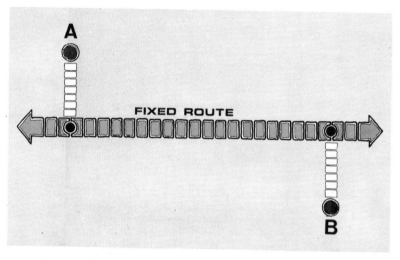

Figure 2-2.
The fixed-route system. Drawing by Don Evans.

esting short-range (neighborhood scale) fixed-route system was used in the Swiss National Exposition of 1964 and in Montreal's EXPO '67 and in other expositions: The Minitrain. The Minitrain is a small, electrically powered, lightweight train that travels on a lightweight rail system, and is quite adaptable as a circulation device within a small area, operating silently enough to be routed through buildings, a fairground gimmick that might prove useful in a high-density housing or business complex. Of course, a short-range fixed-route system is any system with a short routing. City buses, for instance, if routed to circulate within a specific neighborhood, would be acting as a short-range system.

One proposed short-range system for shuttling suburbanites between homes and train stations is called "Dial-A-Bus." Small

Figure 2-3.
A minibus. Photo by author.

(eight-to-twenty-passenger) buses would respond as a door-to-door collector to directions from a computer, which would receive telephone calls from commuters desiring service, and would "continuously optimize the routes of the buses in transit for speedy responses to the developing demand."[1]

More commonly, however, the city bus is used as a medium-

1. *Scientific American,* July 1969, p. 21.

range fixed-route system. It is used in an intracity capacity, with routes moving each vehicle across the whole metropolitan area, as opposed to restricting it to a single neighborhood. City buses, trolleys, and subways, conventional and new, are all medium-range fixed-route systems.

Figure 2-4.
Typical city bus. Photo by author.

Long-range fixed-route systems are those that operate between cities. The conventional freight and passenger railroads are long-range fixed-route systems, as are the new high speed passenger rail systems, such as Penn Central's Metroliner (120 mph), which runs between Washington and Philadelphia and New York.

Fixed-route systems are currently the subject of a significant amount of engineering attention, especially in the medium- and long-range categories. We are constantly exposed to articles on the advantages of steel wheels on steel tracks, or rubber wheels on concrete tracks, or sustaining an air cushion between

Figure 2-5.
New generation of transit vehicles (BART) contrasted with the past generation (cable car). Courtesy Bay Area Rapid Transit District.

the vehicle and the tracks, or, similarly, holding the vehicle off the tracks by magnetic repulsion. The Department of Transportation has recently revealed a prototype high speed rail vehicle powered by a linear induction motor, which combined with an air cushion track system, would allow vehicle speeds of

250 mph, similar in concept to a linear induction system developed in Lyons, France, known as "Urba." We also regularly see photos of full-scale "Rapid Transit" vehicle models in association with the installation of new medium-range fixed-route systems in this country, as in San Francisco, Washington, and Seattle, and with the upgrading of existing systems, as in Boston and New York.

We are a gadget-loving people, and we tend to pay attention when we are shown a sleek and comfortable-looking transit vehicle and are told that this device will zip down the rails at twice the possible speed of the family automobile. We are all subject to discomfort at peak load times in the automobile/roadway (random-route) system, and are vaguely aware that things are getting worse instead of better with that system—so we naturally enough look hopefully for the new transportation technology to rescue us from our rush hour traffic jams.

However, with an exception I will discuss shortly, developments in transportation technology can still be categorized into fixed-route or random-route terminology. We cannot intelligently apply our technological gains to the physical environment without knowing the fundamental characteristic of the systems involved: all fixed-route systems share certain common characteristics, as do all random-route systems . . . only by such classifications can we get a handle on the subject.

It is almost accurate to say that the random-route system moves vehicles, the fixed-route system people. The validity of this observation is demonstrated by the following chart from Gottman's *Megalopolis*:[2]

The fixed-route system not only carries more people through a given point at a given time, it disembarks only people at a destination point. Conversely, the random-route system places

2. Jean Gottman, *Megalopolis* (Cambridge, Mass.: M.I.T. Press, 1961), p. 652.

THE AMERICAN TRANSIT ASSOCIATION HAS PRODUCED THE
FOLLOWING ESTIMATES OF CARRYING CAPACITIES
OF SINGLE LANES, PER HOUR

Passengers in autos on surface streets	1,575
Passengers in autos on elevated highways	2,025
Passengers in buses on surface streets	9,000
Passengers in streetcars on surface streets	13,500
Passengers in streetcars in subways	20,000
Passengers in local subway trains	40,000
Passengers in express subway trains	60,000

both vehicles and passengers at the destination point, the vehicles demanding parking space while the passenger carries on his activities as a pedestrian. In a noncentralized area such as a conventional suburban housing area, the parking requirements of the random-route system can be handled (although not necessarily pleasantly); in a centralized area, especially a high-density area, the parking requirements are all too great, demanding entire buildings devoted to temporary vehicle storage, as well as every available piece of open land, including curb spaces on all the streets. In this situation the fixed-route system moves only people into an area, since the fixed-route vehicles (including buses) stay on the system. (There are certain random-route vehicles that act in this latter capacity, such as delivery vehicles, taxis, and emergency vehicles, none of which demand long-term parking.)

By the very nature of the systems, the random-route system demands relatively huge amounts of landspace as compared to the fixed-route system, especially when we add in the support systems, such as parking lots, garages, gas stations, and the like, the total landspace of which dwarfs the comparable space required for fixed-route railyards, terminal buildings, etc. Also, in terms of right-of-way landspace for each system, it should be obvious that the cross-sectional area of an expressway must be many times greater than the cross-sectional area of a subway to carry the same number of people past a point during the same amount of time. This becomes significant when we become concerned with the environmental implications of con-

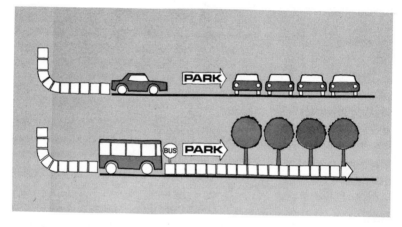

Figure 2-6.
The destination point for the random-route system must accommodate both people and parked automobiles. Drawing by Don Evans.

structing an elevated or ground-level urban expressway as opposed to a buried subway.

There is also a basic difference between system types regarding control over traffic flow on each system. Random-route system traffic engineers expend a great deal of energy on the problem of keeping commuter automobiles on the move, primarily by systemizing traffic signals. However, the fixed-route system lends itself to total control, not partial control, when automated and computerized. This is known as automatic train control (ATC), and is currently in operation with the "Metro" in Montreal, the "Municipal Subway II" in Barcelona, "Line II" of the Paris "Metro," the BARTD system, and the Westinghouse "Transit Expressway." [3] What this means is that the total system can be operated automatically from a centralized point,

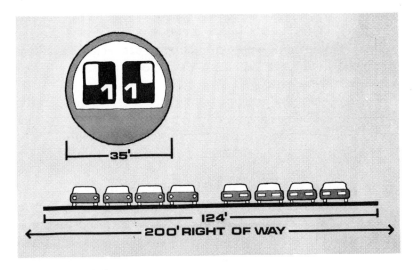

Figure 2-7.
Two-lane local subway contrasted with eight-lane expressway. One lane of the subway can carry 40,000 people per hour, contrasted with 2,625 people in one lane of the expressway. The expressway would require thirty-two lanes to equal the capacity of the two-lane subway. The fixed-route system, due to its small cross-sectional area, can be buried when desired, an option not practical with the random-route system.

using a computerized master board. This, keyed with an extensive route-desire notification system (usually activated by ticket purchase or token deposit, or by turning a turnstile in the

3. Ralph Warburton, "Systems Design for Urban Transit," *Journal of the Franklin Institute,* November 1968, p. 541.

station) allows the weighting of train sizes and schedules to fit load demands. With an ATC vehicle that has its own motive source, such as Westinghouse's Transit Expressway vehicle, the vehicle can be moved about the system to meet load demands either as an individual vehicle (which would be quite useful to meet movement demands to places not drawing large crowds), or it can be linked into trains, as circumstances dictate.

Probably the most important difference between the random-route and fixed-route systems is the type of physical environment each best serves.

The random-route system most effectively serves low-density, widely spread, noncentralized activity areas on a door-to-door basis, such as among suburban housing tracts. Conversely, it is least effective in a centralized situation, for the vehicular congestion that occurs there greatly decreases the advantages of route-selection at random, and inhibits smooth traffic flow.

On the other hand, fixed-route systems run from station to station (be that station a simple bus stop or Grand Central), and operates most efficiently when the stations serve great numbers of passengers, which means centralized areas. Fixed-route systems are least effective in low-density areas, where passengers are scattered. Fixed-route systems, when they are railed, have an advantage over random-route systems in that they operate on exclusive rights-of-way and are not subject to jam-ups due to traffic congestion.

In this sense, the random-route and fixed-route systems complement each other: the random-route system works best in decentralized areas, and is handicapped in centralized areas; and the fixed-route system best serves centralized areas, and cannot easily serve decentralized areas.

The fact that the operational characteristics of each system type can complement the other, in terms of providing transportation coverage throughout a physical environment that includes both centralized and noncentralized, high-density and low-density conditions, is significant. The fact that these system types are not now planned or operated on a complementary basis, and do not provide adequate, appropriate, and comprehensive service to the urban and suburban environment, is critical. This book proposes to demonstrate not only why these dual systems must be planned as a complementary total system, but also how this could and should be accomplished, revealing along the way the benefits of doing so.

I do not wish to neglect certain transportation proposals that would have the same vehicle participate in both fixed-route and random-route capacities. One of the most commonly proposed is the "automation" of the automobile/roadway system. That is, each vehicle would become, in effect, a robot: the passenger would select a destination-point by one method or another, and the vehicle would proceed to that point, following guidance devices in the roadbed, or by mounting rails, moving safely due to collision-avoidance devices on board.[4] The elimination of drivers from automobiles would unquestionably be the greatest safety innovation since the electric razor. Another possible boon would accrue if the automobile could dump its passengers at their destinations, and then proceed back home to await recall, thus eliminating parking requirements at the destination points. A further refinement of this system would be to have all the vehicles parked at municipal garages at all times, awaiting calls, and never parking at any destination-points. This type of system could relieve us from one of our greatest problems of the automobile/roadway system: the vast amounts of urban landspace we must devote to parking in places where other land-uses are desired. It does not, however, help us reduce the size and number of expressways

4. John J. O'Mara, "Automatic Control of Traffic," *Traffic Safety* 68 (November 1968): 8.

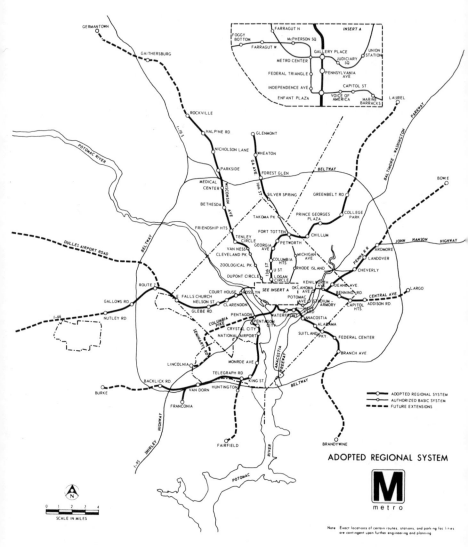

Figure 2-8.
Metro system layout. Courtesy Washington Metropolitan Area Transit Authority.

that are destroying the environment, and shows us no solution to peak-traffic problems.

I am not dismissing such proposals solely because they do not fit neatly into the proposed categories. I simply feel that such a hybrid device is not necessarily as desirable as it might seem. It would possess few of the advantages of a true fixed-route system, such as large passenger capacity, and would be hauling around a great deal of expensive fixed-route gear when operating as a random-route vehicle. Integrating such a dual system into the environment would also be tricky in both functional and land-use planning terms. For example, how would we decide which roadbeds to automate, and which not? While acknowledging that this is a transportation choice, I am focusing discussion on those system types with which we have experience, in both operation and environment effectiveness, on the grounds that our experience in these areas with these systems will allow us predictable results when dealing with them.

This is not to imply that the conventional fixed-route systems do not have problems, or that we handle them properly. Conventional bus systems are fixed-route systems, but have the disadvantage of having to move within the random-route system, competing with automobiles. A much hailed attempt at providing the buses with exclusive rights-of-way, such as providing exclusive bus lanes (as is presently under trial on the Shirley Highway in Washington, D.C.), is intended to prolong the life of the bus as an intra-urban transportation device. Though useful, it is limited to the long stretches outside the high-density areas. The automobile demand on most urban streets is far too great to allow such exclusive lanes.

A most interesting variation on the railed transit theme has been proposed by the General Research Corporation of Santa Barbara, California. Described as "personal transit," very small (two-to-four-passenger) electrically powered vehicles would

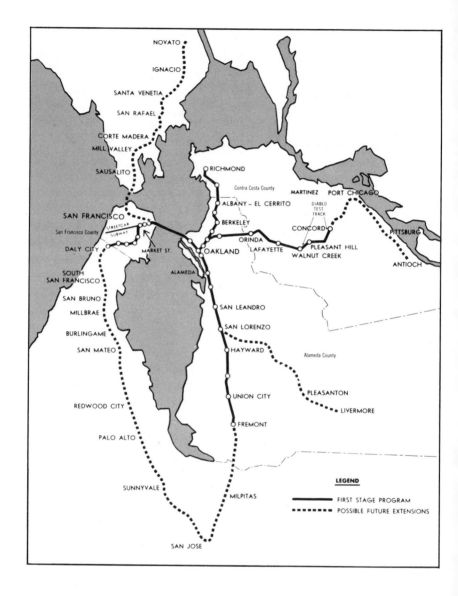

Figure 2-9.
BART system layout. Courtesy Bay Area Rapid Transit District.

ride the rail system instead of large multipassenger cars. The passenger would board the vehicle at a station, punch out his destination desires on a keyboard, and be delivered to the selected station without transfers. Based on computer-model studies of a hypothetical application of "personal transit" to

Figure 2-10.
Metro station entrance, Dupont Circle. Courtesy Washington Metropolitan Area Transit Authority.

Boston, this group of systems analysts highly recommends such a system to accommodate future movement needs, and suggests that development of "personal transit" systems could be rapidly and cheaply accomplished.[5] While discussion of railed transit systems in this book has centered on more conventional (train type) forms, the "personal transit" concept is certainly

5. *Scientific American,* July 1969, p. 21.

compatible with the expressed theme, and should be kept in mind.

It is worth noting that the fixed-route and random-route systems have another difference in operating characteristics: the random-route system is a source of air pollution and accidents

Figure 2-11.
Metro station entrance, Judiciary Square. Courtesy Washington Metropolitan Area Transit Authority.

on a scale so great that the system is a threat to man—the fixed-route system (which is electrically powered, as all modern systems are) poses no parallel threats.

Automobiles play a significant role in the atmosphere poisoning business; in New York automobiles account for 33 percent of the bad air, in Washington 50 percent, and in Los Angeles 90 percent.[6] "Every city in the United States with a population

6. Richard Hall, "Pollution," *Life Magazine*, February 7, 1969, p. 59.

of over 50,000 has—or is about to have—a photochemical smog problem due to its automobiles."[7] Of course, the automobiles share the blame with heavy industry, and as recently noted in *Time* magazine, with the jet airliners, each of which dumps a quantity of pollution equal to that of a thousand cars.[8] How-

Figure 2-12.
Metro station interior, Judiciary Square. Courtesy Washington Metropolitan Area Transit Authority.

ever, there are many thousands of communities in this country that have neither heavy industry nor jet airliner traffic, but every one of them is saturated with automobiles.

   . . . In the last three years, Detroit has been struggling sincerely with the problem of reducing contaminants in automobile exhaust. Manufacturers claim that their '68 and '69

7. Ibid.
8. *Time*, January 5, 1970.

engines are meeting the recently adopted Federal Emission Standard of 275 ppm of hydrocarbons, but the increasing numbers of cars threaten to cancel out the reduction.

California's example is instructive. Beginning with 1966 models, State laws set exhaust emission standards at 275 ppm hyrocarbons, and 1.5 percent carbon monoxide and, at least in theory, permit no cars to be sold in the state which exceed these limits. Test facilities were set up to check samples of new cars, and highway patrolmen were empowered to stop smoke-belching vehicles and give their drivers $25 summonses. Despite these stringent measures, the soaring car population in Los Angeles has all but nullified their effectiveness. Automobiles still spew 12,000 tons of wastes into the Los Angeles air each day, as against 13,000 a day when the program began.

"If it weren't for the automobiles," says Louis J. Fuller, head of Los Angeles County's Air Pollution Agency, "we'd have the finest air quality of any major population area in the world." Right now, Los Angeles has the fourth dirtiest air in the nation—behind New York, Chicago, and Philadelphia.[9]

The fact that over fifty thousand people die each year in the United States[10] in our random-route system is distressing; some might claim it is intolerable. Disabling injuries for the first nine months of 1968 are estimated at 1.4 million cases, and the cost of motor-vehicle accidents for the same period is estimated at $9 billion.[11]

The physical hazards demonstrated by these statistics are inherent in the random-route system; the number of decisions and responses that must be made by the operator is at certain critical times far beyond the capability of the human being, regardless of his training and physical fitness. People die when

9. Hall, "Pollution," p. 59.
10. J. L. Recht, "The Traffic Record," *Traffic Safety* 69 (January 1969): 28–29.
11. Ibid.

these conditions occur. Training programs, traffic rules, and signals are most effective when traffic is slow and of a very low density—when the numbers of decisions are within the operator's capabilities. High speeds and high densities of traffic, typical peak hour conditions on any urban expressway,

Figure 2-13.
Metro station interior, 12th & G, NW. Courtesy Washington Metropolitan Area Transit Authority.

increase dramatically the numbers of variables to be dealt with by the operator.

It might be argued that air pollution and driving hazards are basically technicalities, subject to pending revisions. The automobile industry teases us with electrically-powered and steam-powered proposals (each nonpollutant), simultaneously explaining why they cannot be produced at this time. Ralph Nader's public debates with industry representatives on the subject of vehicle safety features have laid bare the industry attitudes toward developing "safe" vehicles—making it clear that the industry would produce only those safety features forced upon it by legislation. The industry has not produced pollution control devices out of a sense of public duty, either.

Figure 2-14.
BART MacArthur station (model). Courtesy Bay Area Rapid Transit District.

Ford and Chrysler have been discovered to be actively discouraging sales of their pollution control devices (required by California law) outside California, primarily by tying them to delayed delivery dates.[12] The automobile industry is based on economic competition; each company must produce the most

12. Jack Anderson, "Washington Merry-Go-Round," *The Washington Post,* February 26, 1970.

salable product to survive, and safety devices and pollution control devices, which increase the purchase price of the vehicle, are low priority items with the buying public. For most Americans, exchanging the family V-8 for a steam or electric automobile is an amusing thought—and to do so solely on the basis that the old gasoline buggy was fouling up the air is beyond serious discussion. A parallel attitude accompanies conjecture about a "safe" automobile, since that vehicle would most likely retain few of those design features we grow to know and love, style-year after style-year.

Without a large market for pollution-proof and accident-proof vehicles, the automobile industry has little impetus to

Figure 2-15.
BART MacArthur station, under construction in an expressway right-of-way.

commit itself to the unquestionably expensive task of developing and mass producing them. Theoretically, such vehicles could be legislated into existence. However, such legislation cannot be written without the support of the public, and since it is the public that would bear the burden of this in terms of escalated purchase costs, the prospects of seeing a nonpollutant accident-proof vehicle on the streets anytime soon, as the result of a market demand or legislation, are mighty slim.

Meanwhile, the problems do not go away. Beyond the immediate threat of pollution-induced respiratory diseases, fuel-produced carbon dioxide accumulated in the atmosphere works, as does glass, as a "greenhouse"—it passes visible light but absorbs infrared rays.

> Carbon dioxide makes a huge greenhouse of the earth, allowing sunlight to reach the earth's surface but limiting reradiation of the resulting heat into space . . . the extra heat due to fuel-produced carbon dioxide accumulated in the air by the year 2000 might be sufficient to melt the Antarctic Ice Cap—in 4000 years according to one report, or in 400 according to another. . . . "The melting of the Antarctic Ice Cap would raise sea level by 400 feet" . . . this would result in catastrophe for much of the world's inhabited land and many of its major cities.[13]

Since we seemingly cannot be prodded into significant auto-safety action by the fact that the random-route system claims over 50,000 lives each year, it is probably foolish to suppose that large-scale sympathy can be worked up for the world air pollution situation four or more centuries from now. (It should be noted, however, that if most of our daily commuter-type movement activities were conducted within a fixed-

13. Barry Commoner, *Science and Survival* (New York: The Viking Press, Inc., Compass Edition, 1967), p. 11.

route, instead of random-route, system, pollution and safety problems would be greatly reduced as significant problems.)

At present the correlation between fixed-route and random-route system planning is almost nonexistent. More particularly, the random-route vehicle, the automobile, is produced as a

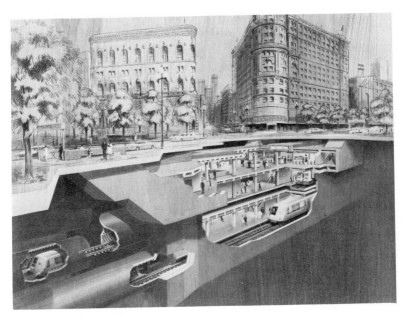

Figure 2-16.
BART Powell Street station (cutaway). Courtesy Bay Area Rapid Transit District.

consumer item, to be purchased and operated by the passenger, as opposed to the fixed-route vehicle, on which rides are purchased, but not the vehicle itself. Obviously, this economic factor plays a role in setting design standards for the different vehicle types. In fact, an interesting design cycle has occurred because of this.

When the railed transit systems were first installed in this country, in the late 1800s, their utility value far outstripped any competition, which was horse-drawn if not pedestrian. Therefore, they were designed with passenger numbers, instead of passenger comfort, in mind. As the automobile industry boomed in the twentieth century, and millions of automobiles were produced, each auto maker in hot competition with the other in terms of performance, comfort, and style, the transit systems were soon left far behind in offering personal amenities. And so, these transit systems began to be used only by those compelled to use them, for utilitarian or economic reasons. These systems were not in a position to upgrade themselves progressively, as public transportation monies were almost totally committed to the nationwide expansion of the roadway network. Only now, when traffic congestion heralds a forthcoming breakdown of the random-route system in urban areas, do we see transit vehicles paraded before the public, marketed on other than strictly utilitarian grounds. Unlike the random-route system, which has had unquestioning and overwhelming support from government and industry for a half century, the fixed-route systems must approach the public coffers with hat in hand, in competition with the random-route system.

Competition between the system types for public funds has not proved advantageous in terms of providing responsible comprehensive transport. Significantly, the organizers, planners, supporters, and backers of the random-route system in this country are a completely separate body of people from their counterparts associated with fixed-route systems. And these two bodies of special interests are usually only casually associated with the various public and private land-use planning agencies in a selected urban area.

These facts take on meaning when we begin to realize that the operational differences between random- and fixed-route systems are not only significant in terms of the functional

Figure 2-17.
BART Powell Street station, under construction. Courtesy Bay Area Rapid Transit District.

aspects of transporting people around the urban environment; the differences themselves play an active (but poorly appreciated) role in determining the character and distribution of land-use activities within and about the urban environment.

I hope to demonstrate that transportation handling has a dual responsibility—that of concern for efficient and desirable operations, and that of recognizing the environmental implications of the particular system used.

Three

FUNCTIONAL PROBLEMS

THE LAND TRANSPORTATION STORY in this country in the 1900s has been the dramatic and unparalleled development and growth of the random-route system. Almost total commitment to this system type over the years has led to some critical problems . . . problems related to the operational or functional aspects of the system, and problems related to the influence the system has had over the form of development of the physical environment. I will outline the most outstanding functional problems in this chapter, and discuss the environmental ones in the next.

Two functional problems with the random-route system are growing at a scale approaching crisis proportions: traffic congestion and urban parking.

We have over 90 million vehicles on the road, with 2.8 million more added each year, *a growth rate three times greater than the national population increase.*[1] Obviously, these vehicles must be accommodated with parking spaces at every destination—be that destination in an area that can handle them or not.

1. Richard Hall, "Pollution," *Life Magazine*, February 7, 1969, p. 50.

Every urban area is subject to a daily tide-like movement of automobiles, entering the high-density work areas together in the mornings, leaving for the low-density residential areas together in the evenings. As we all know, these commuter movement cycles are peak congestion periods, and are often great traffic jam periods, due to the great frequency of accidents that occur.

To keep the traffic flowing we commit 70 percent of the activities of our state and local law enforcement agencies to traffic-related duties.[2] We conduct continuous construction programs to modify and expand our roadway systems to accommodate peak traffic loads, at monumental expense. Yet, it is hard to point out any urban expressway, new or old, that is not congested at peak load times. The number of vehicles is quite simply growing at a much faster rate than the roadway network—traffic congestion cannot help but become progressively worse.

Similarly, the landspace within city centers is a finite thing. As the population grows, landspace once available for parking becomes necessary for buildings, during a time when the parking demands are growing by leaps and bounds. (It is estimated that an automobile parked in downtown Toronto while its owner is at work is occupying $30,000 to $40,000 worth of land —and one-third of downtown Toronto is devoted to the automobile.)[3] Urban expressways are constructed and/or expanded to satisfy the great and growing access demands, ironically dumping more and more vehicles into landspace that simply cannot handle all of them.

This might not seem to be a system with a very healthy

2. Drew Pearson and Jack Anderson, "Washington Merry-Go-Round," *The Washington Post*, December 17, 1968.

3. G. Warren Heenan, "Rapid Transit and Property Value," *Community Planning Review*, Spring 1967, p. 5.

future . . . and it's not. The numbers of vehicles are increasing beyond the capacity of the roadways and the parking spaces. It is a small risk to predict major system breakdowns in certain urban areas, in the form of massive long-term traffic jams.

We assume that there is enough expertise in our traffic management, traffic engineering, and roadbuilding agencies to prevent the overall automobile/roadway system from becoming less functional than it is now. However, a look at system planning techniques might indicate that the assumption is not necessarily correct.

The prevailing roadbuilding philosophy is one of continually providing better and better access, wherever such access is indicated as necessary. In order to do this, the existing roadway system is subject to constant monitoring (cordon counts). This pulse-taking establishes not only congestion build-up patterns, but also overall "desire lines of travel," which is to say that the roadways utilized by significant traffic loads (primarily daily commuter movements) can be identified. On the basis of current congestion problems on these roadways, as well as that of population (automobile) growth projections, roadbuilding programs are laid out.

For the most part, this is simply a matter of boosting the sizes of existing roadways by adding additional lanes. However, quite often flow patterns will build up in areas without existing street configurations appropriate to the loads, or readily adaptable (by expansion) to the loads. The most normal result of this set of circumstances is that the area in question is subject to a great amount of property clearance for an on-grade or elevated expressway. After all, continual traffic flow is the priority consideration here.

The random-route system planner is in a dilemma, though. His responsibility is to keep the traffic flowing, which means that he must constantly massage the total roadway system to eliminate bottlenecks. The development of the cloverleaf intersection has been hailed for years as an innovative traffic-flow handler, as has more recently the installation in some cities of computer-coordinated signal lights. For the most part, however, this is not an innovative task; the problem is that of handling a quickly growing automobile population on a road system that cannot grow as quickly, as indicated by the fact that with the exception of the interstate highway system, most current roadbuilding is in the area of urban expressways, either expanding existing routes or developing new ones.

The problem here is twofold: (1) The goal of providing universal accessibility (meaning peak loads) for automobile traffic flow is most likely not achievable, as long as the automobile population sustains its growth rate, regardless of how much urban and suburban landspace we commit to roadways (some highway planners seem to recognize no limits to this commitment); and (2) this goal, whether achievable or not, neglects the problem of handling parked automobiles at those points made so accessible. Watching our random-route system agencies frantically building expressways in order to funnel great and growing numbers of automobiles into densely packed urban activity centers, where the parked automobile is the least desirable from any standpoint of land use, reminds me of the old Texas adage regarding the dubious prospects of trying to place twenty pounds of manure into a ten-pound gunny sack.

For the most part, our roadbuilding philosophy is a reactionary one. We not only disregard the environmental implications of our roadways, but we do not think through our function-oriented planning in a comprehensive manner.

Probably the most enlightened concept in random-route system planning in the last few years is that of establishing perimeter parking lots around high-density activity areas. In this concept, the suburban commuter drives in to a peripheral parking lot, parks his automobile, boards a bus, and rides in to his job. A sophisticated use of peripheral parking has been suggested by Architect Louis Kahn for Philadelphia. Kahn surrounds the high-density central business district (CBD) of Philadelphia with expressways and limits automobile access to the CBD to entering municipal parking towers which would form entrance-points to the CBD. The interior area of the CBD would be limited to service vehicles, public transit, and pedestrian movement.

> The tower entrances and interchanges, wound-up parking terminals, suggest a new stimulus to unity in urban architecture, one which would find expression from the order of movement. The location and design of these entrances are an integral part of the design of the expressway. At night we know these towers by their illumination in color. These yellow, red, green, blue and white towers tell us the sector we are entering, and along the approach, light is used to see by and to give us direction.[4]

As planned, this proposal would allow the CBD to re-orient much of its landspace from automobiles to pedestrians, which is totally desirable in any high-density area.

Unfortunately, we are slow to institute such a concept on a working basis. Philadelphia did not institute Kahn's scheme, but Washington, D.C. has dabbled with the experiment: commuters approaching the District from certain directions have the option of leaving their automobiles in parking lots and boarding buses. The flaw here is that the system is totally voluntary—the bus the commuter boards must fight its way

4. Alison Smithson and Peter Smithson, *Urban Structuring* (New York: Reinhold Publishing Corp., 1967), p. 45.

into the District in the middle of all the traffic that did not choose to park. As long as urban parking is available in the District, and not too expensive, the fringe lots will not be too effective. Of course, urban parking is not infinitely available, and is becoming progressively more expensive.

It is worth noting that when peripheral parking is placed near the destination point (the urban center) the density of automobiles to be parked is great. The same amount of parking, if scattered further out, could be handled in much smaller "packages," sparing us the prospect of having our major urban spaces surrounded by dense rings of parked automobiles.

The amount of urban landspace we can afford to commit to the routing and parking demands of the random-route system is limited. If we do not choose to draw the line now, and seek alternate solutions, while there are features of the urban scene still worth saving, the line will be drawn for us when we have simply saturated, to the point of stopping-up, the urban landscape with automobile parking structures and triple-decked urban expressways. The tail is wagging the dog: we, in the process of attempting to sustain functionality in a transportation system that is supposed to serve us, are not making it more functional, but instead, are boosting its capacity for environmental destruction.

As I have said, the random-route system planner is in a dilemma. He is trying to solve problems that are a product of the system itself. Of course, an alternate to the random-route system for resolving the functional flow problems is a large-scale commitment to the fixed-route system. This is not to say that the contemporary fixed-route system planner has an automatically superior approach—but, as I will demonstrate, he does have options with his system that are not available with the random-route system—options with positive land-use planning benefits.

However, as it stands, fixed-route systems in the United States are very restricted in the scope of their layouts, due to the extremely small economic investment we make in them. They usually structure themselves to provide the most for the money allotted them, but it is usually not enough to allow them to fulfill their potential on a functional level, much less an environmental level.

I am speaking here of the railed, medium-range systems, notably the new ones, such as in Seattle, San Francisco, and Washington, D.C. Bus systems share the handicap of limited funds, but are also handicapped in another way which immensely decreases their functional ability as a movement device: they share the random-route roadway system, meaning that they must struggle in automobile traffic. (Railed systems have exclusive right-of-way, which means that control over the movement patterns is possible within the system. For the most part, when I discuss fixed-route system planning, I am speaking of railed systems.)

If, as I believe, we are forced to recognize that we must seek an alternate to the random-route system (for commuter movements), and if we determine that the best possible alternate is the fixed-route system, we must be prepared to commit ourselves to this system on a level greater than attempted anywhere before.

The functional limitations of the random-route system outline a basic argument against its perpetuation in its present form. Let us take a look now at the environmental aspects of our contemporary transportation methods.

Four

ENVIRONMENTAL PROBLEMS

To APPRECIATE PROPERLY the role of the random-route system in the environment, we must understand how this system has participated in the formation of the environment since its introduction at the beginning of the century.

During this century, the random-route system has played a dominant role in shaping the environment as we know it, since it made possible, through the mass ownership of automobiles and the vast and growing network of roadways: the physical separation by long distances of an individual's place of work and place of residence, as well as places of shopping and entertainment; the opportunity to reside in spread-out low-density housing areas; and the horizontal growth of urban concentrations to the extent that what we once called the city we now must call a metropolitan area, due to its inclusion of many smaller, formerly outlying, communities. We are even seeing metropolitan areas growing into region-sized entities.

The pre-automobile turn-of-the-century American city was basically constructed for pedestrians. It was characterized by high-density living and working facilities, since the daily life-patterns of most individuals were conducted on foot. The only range-extenders of these life-patterns were the horse and buggy, and the fixed-route systems of the day: the trolley and the subway (in certain cities). There was a suburb, usually composed of those wealthy enough to afford the required mobility . . . suburbs which inspired crowded city dwellers with images of living-styles that the automobile later freed them to seek. However, the total preautomobile city was a relatively still environment, in terms of overall motion. The patrons of the transit systems of the day were generally moving from high-density housing areas to high-density work areas, living at a distance not so much from choice, but because, in those pre-high-rise days, those high-density housing areas within pedestrian range of workplaces were simply saturated. Another characteristic of this era was the fully developed neighborhood, a neighborhood typified by bottom-floor shops with residents above, home industries, and the like. Each neighborhood had a distinct identity, as most of the people living within the neighborhood worked there, were entertained there, shopped there, were schooled there, and for the most part, never had many reasons for leaving there. The remains of these neighborhood areas still exist in our older cities, housing now for the most part the impoverished, the illiterate, and the racially oppressed.

There is little about the preautomobile turn-of-the-century city that demands nostalgia, however. These cities had to absorb population growth by increasing their physical densities, as the limitations of travel-range prohibited horizontal expansion. The automobile appeared on the scene when the crowding of the city, combined with the alleged wholesomeness of rural life, made it valuable as an escape device. Suburban living, for so long only the option of the wealthy, became the option for the masses, or at least the middle-class. One could have his cake and eat it too, by working in the city and living in the semicountry. The automobile/roadway system dramatically extended the range of the life patterns of the urban American.

The random-route system was built up in a rather simple manner. Since the preauto city was patterned on a street system, the primary new roadway building occurred outside the city, expanding or building anew the road connections between cities. As the automobile made the landscape surrounding the city more accessible to those living within the city, agricultural land adjacent to the intercity highways became more valuable for laying out streets and houseplots than for farming. The preauto city became surrounded with a ring of low-density housing. "From 1900 until 1920 central cities were growing faster than their tributary rings. However, in each decade since 1920 the rings have been growing faster than the central cities. Thus, the comparative growth rates between central cities and their rings have now become considerable. In the decade between 1940 and 1950, rings grew almost two and a half times as fast as central cities." [1] Between 1960 and 1970, central cities grew by only 0.7 million while the suburbs grew by 15.1 million, giving the suburbs the majority of residents (69.6 million in suburbs, 58.5 million in central cities, by the latest census). Of course, the suburban rings are not exclusively residential, as branch banks, supermarkets, and department stores began to follow the trade out into the rings as early as the 1930s, as did the school systems. As suburbia grew, so did the commercial activities, developing into the now familiar shopping centers and commercial strips.

We traditionally associate the word "urban" with the city; "suburban" with low-density single-family dwellings surrounding the city; and "rural" with land occupied with wilderness or

1. William M. Dobriner, *Class in Suburbia* (Englewood Cliffs, N.J.: Prentice-Hall, Inc., 1963), p. 146.

agricultural activities. We traditionally equate the city with high-density living patterns, with activities highly interrelated with suburbia, and to a much lesser extent, with the rural surroundings. The hierarchy has for years seemed quite straightforward, and has been assumed to be a natural beginning point for analysis. However, within the last decade, more and more urbanologists have been recognizing the multicity relationships described by Jean Gottman in *Megalopolis*.[2] This concept reveals that two or three or more cities, within a hundred or so miles of each other, become in effect a continuous urban entity. This occurs as the suburban developments which surround each city expand, mainly along the best access routes.

The cities grow toward each other in a rather spontaneous (that is, unplanned) manner; this growth encompassing those small communities, as well as rural and industrial areas, in the spaces between the cities.

Gottman has concentrated on the greatest complex of this sort in the world: the development in the Northeastern United States extending from the Allegheny Mountains on the west to the Atlantic on the east, Boston on the north to Washington on the south, including Boston, New York, Philadelphia, Baltimore, Washington, and the hundreds of smaller communities in between, giving this complex the name "Megalopolis." Although this is the largest (in population) of this type of development, it is certainly not the only such development in the country.

> According to a study made by *U.S. News & World Report* (September 18, 1961) the thirteen major "strip cities" in the United States—Boston to Washington, Albany to Erie, Cleveland to Pittsburgh, Toledo to Cincinnati, Detroit to Muskegon,

2. Jean Gottman, *Megalopolis* (Cambridge, Mass.: M.I.T. Press, 1961), p. 652.

Chicago-Gary to Milwaukee, St. Louis to Peoria, Seattle to Eugene, San Francisco to San Diego, Kansas City to Sioux Falls, Fort Worth-Dallas-San Antonio-Houston, Miami-Tampa-Jacksonville, and Atlanta to Raleigh—contain half the population of the country (89,395,469) and have increased more than 25 percent from 1950. Of the total 212 metropolitan areas in the nation, 119 fall within 13 giant strip city patterns.

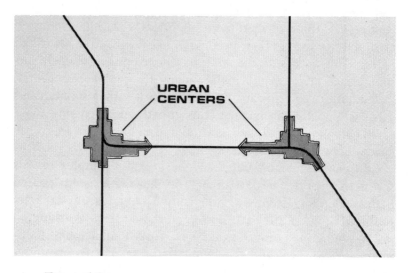

Figure 4-1.
Urban areas inevitably grow toward each other along their interconnecting highways. Drawing by Don Evans.

Not only did half the population live within these supermetropolitan constellations, but 109 billion dollars in retail trade or 54.7 percent of the total consumer market was expended there.[3]

For future reference in this text, I refer to the strip city, or

3. Dobriner, *Class in Suburbia,* p. 150.

Megalopolis, development as the Regional Urban Environment (RUE).

The RUE is a product of the random-route system. The system, of course, cannot take credit for the population growth in this century, or for the many sociological factors which have made the suburbs attractive in this period. It was simply introduced at a time when many of our cities were becoming too crowded to absorb their growing populations without expansion of some sort. (Had the random-route system not come along, this expansion would have occurred in a different manner, most probably that of the formation of many new satellite cities surrounding the original cities, all linked together with fixed-route systems.)

The very nature of the random-route system—that of serving most effectively those activities which are decentralized—dictated the character of suburbia. The point is that land-use configurations must, to a great extent, conform to the nature of the transportation systems that serve them. It is worth noting that the basic character of the urban environment changed in this century without the benefit of any positive plan. No master planner decided that at some moment the cities should spread out into low-density suburbs, and that the way to do so would be to introduce the automobile to the American public on a mass basis, combined with an ambitious road-building industry.

This is not to imply that all that has happened in terms of the development of the urban environment so far is misdirected. I simply wish to point out that a particular transportation system was embraced on its functional merits with little understanding or concern over its environmental implications.

We are not really in a position to continue to let a transportation system act as an environmental form-determinant without a complete understanding of its long-range effects, in terms of desirability. This is of special importance to us as we see the random-route system facing some critical functional problems, and are contemplating possible alternatives.

We face severe land-use problems in this country, and several of them can be attributed to the random-route system, either because of direct functional conflicts with desired land usage, or because undesirable land usage is made possible by the random-route system.

What is so obvious about the random-route system, what is taken so much for granted and so rarely questioned, is the vast amount of landspace in the urban environment that is devoted to roadway usage, as well as for parking and service-activity use. Approximately one-third of the total landspace of Los Angeles is committed to such use, and in the CBD, two-thirds of the landspace is so occupied.[4]

The architectural concessions to the random-route system are enormous. Virtually every residential structure in the United States must provide parking, either in lots or enclosed in the structure, for each family involved, for at least one automobile, and more commonly two. As a general rule, up to one quarter of each suburban house is devoted to sheltering the automobile. High-density apartment structures must often accommodate automobiles internally, in the same proportion, or otherwise stand in a small sea of parked automobiles, or, most commonly, both. In high-density activity areas no piece of open land is safe from automobile parking. Parks and playgrounds lead precarious existences in the face of demands for parking spaces. The conversion of a parking lot into a park or playground is so rare as to be almost unknown in this country; the reverse is not so rare.

Even in preautomobile days most of the landspace between

4. Arthur B. Gallion and Simon Eisner, *The Urban Pattern*, 2nd ed. (Princeton: D. Van Nostrand Co., 1963), p. 308.

the buildings in high-density cities was devoted to roadways, but the difference is that vehicular traffic then was so light and so slow that these streets were comparatively open for pedestrian usage, quite a contrast to the contemporary situation where the pedestrian can only cross the street in reasonable safety by following traffic signals and crossing on marked lines at street intersections. And when an urban expressway cuts through an area, the pedestrian is all but totally blocked from crossing it, the only concession to him being cross-bridges or tunnels, usually miles part. The result, of course, has been the almost total disappearance of the pedestrian except in high-density locations. This condition might be acceptable if the physical surroundings at the various activity nodes in the urban environment were weighted in favor of the pedestrian instead of the automobile. But they aren't.

I do not mean to imply that any pedestrian-oriented area is inherently good. But it makes little sense to sacrifice the interests of the pedestrian in such fundamentally pedestrian-oriented areas as a downtown business and shopping area, or a shopping center. Despite the fantastic array of communications equipment available, we still conduct our most meaningful daily activities as pedestrians. However, we have committed so much landspace to automobile movement and parking spaces that it is not pleasant, convenient or safe to be a pedestrian in most areas. Instead, we move almost entirely indoors to find the safety and quiet required for the accomplishment of our pedestrian-based activities.

An attempt to resolve this in several cities has been the introduction of "shopping malls" in the CBD, that is, closing down key streets to vehicular activities and stocking the "reclaimed" spaces with pedestrian-type amenities (such as benches, fountains, trees, flowers, etc.), refocusing the environment toward the pedestrians who use the area. However, as the total random-route system has not been changed, other factors come into play, factors which have prevented the widespread use of the "mall." Since those people who come to shop or work on this mall must come to it by automobile, the automobile must be parked somewhere. Because as on-street parking on the mall street and off-street parking adjacent to the mall street are eliminated as the mall is constructed, the lost parking spaces must be found on the streets paralleling the mall on both sides. These streets must also handle greater traffic loads as they gain the through-traffic diverted from the mall street. The increased traffic and parking loads on these adjacent streets cause a land-use change there, as some property becomes more valuable for parking structures than for commercial structures. We have here an instance where simply diverting the random-route system to improve land-use conditions in one area creates a corresponding degradation of adjacent areas.

"I like the idea of being able to cross the street safely and not have to worry about inhaling the stinking automobile fumes," is the way Eugene Gladston, a buyer for Mangol's women's clothing store on Lexington Avenue near 58th Street put it. "This could be the greatest thing that happened to this street in the sixteen years that I've been here." In the summer of 1970, in an effort to attain the positive aspects of urban pedestrian malls without the negative, Mayor John Lindsay shut down certain blocks of key streets (Fifth Avenue, Lexington Avenue, Madison Avenue, Eighth Street) on a scheduled one-day-per-week basis. This concept has proved to be quite popular, as people learned that an urban street could be a place for relaxed strolling, football playing, or anything else. "The people have taken over the city! The car is dead, long live the people!" was the reaction of one teenaged appreciator. Only a minority of merchants expressed misgivings about the plan, as some potential customers found the streets more attractive than the shops.

Permanent malls are made almost impossible to have by the existing transportation scene. But the need for such humane urban environments is very much there, so we turn to temporary malls. Not that this is easily done. New York discovered that closing Fifth Avenue and Lexington Avenue simultaneously was impossible, due to the great traffic handling problems that resulted. It is a sad commentary on our times that our streets can only be for people on a rationed basis. Permanent reclamation of significant portions of urban landspace for pedestrian-oriented purposes is very much dependent on finding a method of eliminating the downtown presence of the automobile.

Another attempt at establishing urban outdoor pedestrian spaces has occurred in several sophisticated shopping centers around the country, in which the buildings form a protective ring around a central mall, much in the manner of a wagon train circled to protect itself from an Indian raid, except that the Indians in this case are the multitudes of parked automobiles surrounding the center. In many cases this enclosed environment is an architectural delight, a diamond in the rough, so to speak, when compared to the surrounding environment. However, this image is tainted by the sea of parked vehicles which surround each of these centers; this sea washing up against the surrounding activity areas (usually suburban housing), blighting them, as it makes them undesirable for their original activities.

Preserving segments of the urban landscape for pedestrian-oriented activities in the face of urban parking and movement demands is only one of the environmental problems posed by the random-route system.

The burst of horizontal low-density commercial and residential developments cannot continue to be seen as a viable method for absorbing population growth indefinitely. The development of the various identifiable RUE's has involved in most cases a basic change in land usage; much of the landspace surrounding and in-between the presuburbia cities had been used for agricultural activities . . . as the regions developed to their contemporary sizes, agricultural land had to yield to suburban residential and commercial activities. Ironically, agricultural acreage has decreased over the period of time when demand for agricultural produce has swelled because of the growing population. (In the last decade the farm population has dropped by 3.1 million while the central cities, suburbs, and smaller towns have added 23.4 million.)

Current census data is divided into two basic categories: metropolitan and nonmetropolitan. The metropolitan population, at 129.2 million, is almost two-thirds of the national total of 200.3 million. An additional half-million is anticipated by the year 2000, the great majority of whom will live in metropolitan areas (regions).

The regions are not, of course, infinite entities that can accept all this growth horizontally, if for no other reason than the growth gobbles up essential recreation and agricultural landspace. Some can provide much more low-density expansion than others, yet even the predominantly low-density development of the Los Angeles RUE is reaching its limits in terms of such continued expansion. The City Planning Department of Los Angeles, in its "Goals and Concepts" Programs, has outlined four possible methods of accommodating higher density developments into its landscape: *centers*—spots thirty high-density urban centers around the region; *dispersion*—scatters greater numbers of smaller cores around; *corridors*—links high-density activity into a large north-south spinal strip; and *low density*—involves a network of strips all over the region . . . each of these concepts to be overlaid on the existing low-density "field" or background.[5]

It is one thing, however, to draw up a selection of land-use concepts, but another altogether to implement a choice, without relating that choice to the transportation types at hand. The *centers* and *dispersion* concepts of concentrating activities into nodes are dependent on the node-forming characteristic of the operating fixed-route system, while the strip concepts, *corridor* and *low density* (as I will demonstrate) are natural products of the random-route system. Unless we are sensitive to transportation/land-use relationships, we are always subject to misaligning land-use goals with system characteristics, and thereby seeing the goals thwarted.

(As the regions grow in population, the original high-density areas still attract people, beyond capacity in many cases. In order to meet the high-density demands, the "Megastructure" concept has been developed. The Megastructure is basically a huge building complex, vertically oriented, that incorporates many hundreds of residential units, and often shopping and entertainment activities as well. Architect Moishe Safde constructed a prototype Megastructure in Montreal as EXPO '67, called "Habitat," using mass production techniques, proving that such a structure could be very desirable as a residential environment. This concept is far too appealing to escape application in the future. Our transportation planning must thus include the thought that several thousand commuters may be departing each of these facilities simultaneously in the mornings, which should indicate that we needn't associate the random-route system with all residential situations.)

Occasionally we run into a discussion of land usage in the United States which points out that we are only using about

5. "Los Angeles," *Architectural Record*, April 1968, p. 186.

10 percent of our total landspace for our commercial and residential activities, and that the answer to the problems of crowding in our urban centers is to decentralize into the vast hinterlands, despite the many geographical and climatic fac-

Figure 4-2.
Prototype residential megastructure, "Habitat." Photo by author.

tors which have precluded such activity in the past. We do see new-towns constructed, but in each case they are located within the agricultural land encompassed by established regions. Each recognized RUE still contains quite a bit of open land—primarily agricultural land. This stands to reason, as the original cities could not have prospered there without the surrounding agricultural support. In most cases, land outside the RUE has not been developed to the extent of supporting cities for the simple reason that the land cannot support cities.

Regional urban environments develop in the most productive landspace. When we infill the RUE's open land with suburban facilities, we simultaneously reduce agricultural activities. Geographer Edward Higbee warns: "Obviously the dynamics of population expansion are fantastically unlimited while the area of land is so finite that sometime within the next few generations the present trends in housing will be modified, or the nation's food supply will be grown on roof tops or window boxes rather than farms as we now think of them. Mathematically there cannot continue to be both population multiplication and land subtraction at present rates without reaching some saturation point." [6]

We also see wilderness areas, coast lines, and other pieces of landscape valuable to man for recreational and inspirational purposes (if left in their natural state) systematically subdivided into housing tracts or occupied for industrial or commercial activities when these areas lie within a RUE. As the region increases in overall density, preserving such areas from being "developed" becomes more and more difficult. The infilling process—the crush for housing by a growing population—has allowed tract developers to spread homes out on once-in-a-decade flood plains and stick them on the sides of California mudhills, many soon sliding back off. Misappropriate land-use is rampant, as land is developed to satisfy immediate market demands, with little care for the future. (For some astute

6. Edward Higbee, *The Squeeze: Cities Without Space* (New York: William Morrow and Co., Apollo Edition, 1965), p. 119.

observations on the infilling process as it is occurring within the Washington-Boston RUE, see William H. Whyte's *The Last Landscape.*)[7]

How are such undisciplined land-use practices made possible? The obvious answer is that we simply do not have comprehensive land-use planning powers over the RUE, since the governing powers are all too fragmented for consolidated action. This is not the only factor, however. Our low-density, meaning land-consuming, methods of accommodating population expansion have been made physically possible only by the random-route transportation system.

Land-use is dependent on accessibility. The key to the problem is the easy accessibility to undeveloped landspace with the random-route system. To convert a rural field to a housing tract, land developers need only to lay out a few streets and attach them to the nearest established roadway . . . since the future residents bring along their own automobiles—their half of the system. As a land-development tool, the random-route system has no parallel, regardless of the desirability of the development in each case.

We fail to control the land-use within the RUE in two ways: first by trying to survive the experiment with a set of weak or nonexistent land-use policies and controls, and second by allowing indiscriminate tapping into the existing roadway system. We only consider the random-route system to be a device for *providing* access, failing to recognize that the *withholding* of access can be a highly effective land-use control.

It is interesting to note that the wildfire-like spread of suburban development à la the random-route system has affected the English landscape also. Planners there have decided the unchecked sprawl is an undesirable element, and have experi-

7. William H. Whyte, *The Last Landscape* (Garden City: Doubleday & Co., Inc., 1966).

mented with the construction of circular parks ("greenbelts") around their cities as part of a "containment" policy: "(1) to check further growth of urban area, (2) to prevent neighboring towns from merging, and (3) to preserve the special character of towns." As a containment tool, the greenbelt has proved a failure: suburban sprawl simply leapfrogs the barrier.[8] This might indicate that attempting to control this problem from just the land-use zoning approach, without allowing for the environmental implications of the prevailing transportation system, is too one-sided to be effective.

The random-route system acts as an active partner in proliferating low-density commercial and residential land usage, whether such proliferation is desirable or not. Geographers and conservationists, watching the unchecked spread of "little boxes" over invaluable agricultural and wilderness landspace, find the proliferation not only undesirable, but threatening.

One land-use "type" that is a direct product of the random-route system is the commercial strip. This is a series of commercial activities strung along a significant arterial roadway, most commonly running through low- or medium-density suburban housing areas. Normally, the primary activities along the roadway are transient-oriented—that is, automobile-related activities (gas stations, drive-in groceries, hamburger stands, etc.), which build up first around major intersections, and then spread along the arteries. As the residential population grows on each side of an artery, and as traffic builds up on it, the commercial activities build up accordingly, serving both the transient market and the surrounding residential market. Strips, with few exceptions, build up on the radial arterials and intercity highways that pass through the suburban "rings," as well as on lateral arterials that link the radials, forming a network

8. Whyte, *The Last Landscape,* p. 156.

of linear commercial developments, the in-between spaces filled with suburban housing.

Arterial roadways through residential areas almost always breed strip commercial developments, whether desired or not, and, significantly, whether zoned against or not. Commuter traffic on the artery makes the property on each side of it increasingly undesirable for residential purposes; the property value drops, and as redevelopment of the land for commercial purposes would prove more lucrative for the owner, he goes to work on the zoning board to obtain a reclassification, which he eventually gets. The point is that prevention of a strip development by land-use zoning alone is futile; restricting a strip of land to a residential classification past the time when a transportation system has made that land unfit for residential use is not realistic, and so we find that land-use zoning tends to realign itself, if only after-the-fact, with actual land usage.

A close look at strip developments within the suburban residential environment shows that most shopping centers develop at the intersection of two or more strips, and that when shopping centers are established within a mile or so of each other, strip commercial activities will invariably develop on the main interconnecting roadway.

Linear commercial activity, when on intercity roadways, out in the open countryside, in the form of "gas/food/lodgings," pose few immediate environmental problems. However, when strips develop in the suburban environment, certain sociological relationships develop also. When a suburban area has its commercial activities localized in a shopping center, it has a focal point for many of the activities of its residents. The shopping center, when developed to the extent of not only harboring shopping activities, but also eating places, motion-picture theaters, and other functions, such as a Post Office, becomes, in fact, a community center, which gives the surrounding residential area a neighborhood identity. When, however, centers grow together into strips, something else happens. The strip, instead of focusing a suburban residential area into a neighborhood, divides it in two, forming a barrier between the halves. True enough, the strip offers the same activity-functions to the area,

Figure 4-3.
Typical commercial strip. Photo by author.

but it falls short in one important category: it does little toward making neighborhoods out of otherwise anonymous suburban residential areas. The typical suburbanite finds himself somewhere between commercial strips, only able to identify where he is by the name with which the developer tagged his particular housing-tract.

Commercial strips are outstanding socio-economic elements

of the suburban environment, whether desirable elements or not . . . and if they are not, the random-route system must face examination, since the strip is a function of that system.

Another area of environmental stress is at the interface between air and ground transportation activities—the air termi-

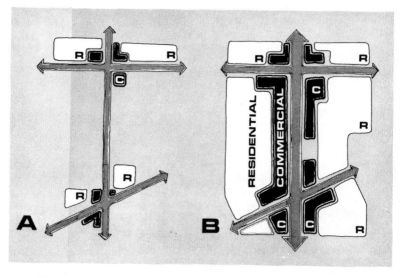

Figure 4-4.
The classical evolution of a commercial strip. A few transient services on a major artery grow into a strip as traffic increases and the surrounding residential areas grow. Drawing by Don Evans.

nal. The quantity of air passengers and air freight moved each year is great and growing, both in intercity and interregional movement. This movement, when occurring at high altitudes and at subsonic speeds, has negligible effects on the region. However, the ground-based focal point for this air activity has significant effects on the region. The scheduled passenger airlines generate extensive ground movement to and from the air terminals, this movement at present being handled almost exclusively by the random-route system.

When air passenger service became established in the 1930s and 1940s, it operated out of the airfields of the pioneering

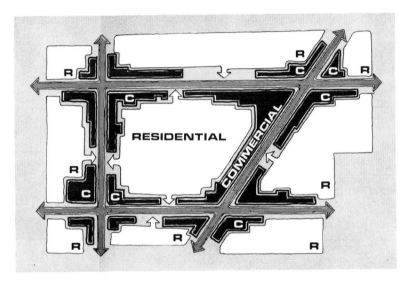

Figure 4-5.
Strip layouts in residential suburbia. Drawing by Don Evans.

days of aviation, built in presuburbia open countryside, relatively close to the major cities. Suburbia, of course, surrounded these airports, placing them in the condition in which we find them today: the size of the aviation industry demands large airports, with extensive waiting spaces for both people and automobiles. Contemporary aircraft technology (meaning jets) demands extended runways, runways which infringe into housing areas, placing extremely loud and potentially hazardous aircraft in close proximity to occupied structures. The airport becomes increasingly incompatible with its surroundings, yet the obvious answer that it should move out to less inhabited surroundings does not work well within the random-route system.

In the Washington, D.C., area, National Airport is located as close as physically possible to the major activity centers. Understandably, this airport is a beehive of both air and ground movement activity. Since National was geographically constrained and physical expansion was impossible where it is located, and since air service demands to the city were growing, the need for a totally new facility in open countryside prompted the construction of Dulles Terminal thirty miles out in the Virginia countryside. This did not, however, constitute a relocation of the National air activities to Dulles. Why? The key to this is ground transportation. Both the crowded and relatively uncomfortable facilities at National are preferred over the efficiency and comfort of the Dulles Terminal because it takes less time to get there—only those living in the Virginia suburbs see a real choice between the airports. In overall terms, the random-route system offers little real choice: the travel time involved in getting to the Dulles Terminal almost defeats the purpose of flying in the first place—speed. Despite the fact that almost half the trip can be made on an expressway, it is still too slow to be considered tolerable by most air travelers.

Moving an airport to empty countryside eliminates many environmental problems, but it cannot be considered satisfactory if quick access to that airport is not made available. Extending an expressway to it seems the answer unless one realizes two things: (1) airport expressways, unless severely restricted in entry points, soon carry more than just airport traffic . . . since they are not sized for additional loads, desired travel times are soon lost; and (2) the expressway acts like any other significant arterial roadway: it "breeds" residential and commercial (strip) activities . . . in effect playing an active role in assuring that the airport will remain in the open countryside only for a short time in the future. Dulles represents both of these factors, although they are not unique to Dulles.

The expressway to Dulles, designed as a no-access thoroughfare, has had suburban developments built up around it (including the new-town of Reston). Access to these areas is basically on old farming roads. The pressure from the commuting residents of this area to have the Dulles road opened up for their use is increasing . . . there is good reason to suspect that much of the housing in that area was constructed in anticipation of that event. A shopping center has already developed on the "town" end of the Dulles road—opening it up to commuter traffic (which seems inevitable) will necessitate frontage roads, which will allow commercial activities to grow out toward Dulles in the classic strip pattern. Of course, opening the Dulles road to commuter traffic will decrease the town-to-airport trip speeds. The Dulles example is typical of all remotely located major airports, except that in most cases, the expressways were never of a limited-access type, and the strips developed more quickly.

Obviously an air terminal must be highly accessible to the area it serves. The trick is to provide access without introducing undesirable land-use changes in the process. One method of doing this would be to connect the airport with other key activity centers with high-speed fixed-route systems, which would not breed strip developments along the routeways (because they could not, without the provision for station-stops) in the process of providing access. It is interesting to note that Cleveland (as well as New York) is currently constructing a downtown/airport rail run, in which air passengers will be able to check their baggage at the downtown terminal, and not have to bother with it again until they get to the other end of their air trip.[9]

Any transportation system has its own unique set of operating characteristics, and these characteristics develop certain relationships with the environment in which the operations occur. In the case of the automobile/roadway system, the operating characteristics, as outlined in the previous chapter, have developed some critical operational problems, problems which threaten the continuance of the system as we know it today. This system has also played an environment-affecting role that has developed some critical environmental problems, problems that demand we reevaluate transportation/environment relationships in terms of immediate and long-range desires.

I want to make clear three points about the Regional Urban Environment before outlining an alternate method of handling regional transportation.

(1) The urban spread, or "sprawl," was made possible (as were the original suburbs) by an extensive network of roads, allowing the vast accessibility, by automobiles, of remote areas, to great numbers of people (the mass ownership of automobiles being long established).

(2) The resultant RUE offers a multitude of choices for living, working, and playing, and having these activities separated or combined, in high-density or low-density spaces. Since the large development called the Regional Urban Environment usually covers hundreds of miles of landspace, it usually encompasses many patches of rural space, sometimes agriculture, sometimes wilderness. The range of living patterns is therefore almost limitless, assuming that the development of the region can be controlled to preserve certain elements from encroach-

9. "Cleveland's Brave Gamble," *Architectural Forum,* November 1968.

ment by other elements, such as selected wilderness areas being destroyed by housing or roadway projects.

(3) The RUE, with its many cities, towns, communities, housing developments, etc., is for all practical purposes under no intelligent control. No city, county, or state can control these regional developments, as they respect no legalistic boundaries, growing as they do across geographic lines as if they weren't there. There are no regional governments with the authority to effect regional planning goals, and even if there were, there is little reason to hope that they could control the region to any greater extent than the various city planning agencies can control the many cities in this country if they follow contemporary planning policies. The only single element in the RUE which can claim a strong cause/effect relationship with the development patterns in the region is transportation. My contention is that transportation is the key to control of the Regional Urban Environment, and that our present transportation policies and techniques are unsatisfactory for this role.

Five

THE PROPOSAL

THE TYPES OF PHYSICAL MOVEMENT that concern us can be generalized into commuter and noncommuter categories. The most common commuter movements are those between home and work in the mornings and work and home in the evenings. These movements are the source of peak congestion problems, as they involve great numbers of people moving simultaneously.

Noncommuter movements are generally those that occur at times other than peak commuter times, and are directed toward other activities, such as shopping, entertainment, and socializing.

Commuter movements are typically between centralized and noncentralized, higher and lower density segments of the environment. The classical commuter flow pattern is that of a suburban ring flowing inward to the urban core in the mornings, radiating outward from the core in the evenings—a tide-like motion. While this pattern still represents most commuter motion, the scene is shifting as the Regional Urban Environments grow into maturity.

This is to say that the generators for commuter movement, the work centers, are no longer all located in the traditional city centers, as we see elements of "clean" industry (manufacturers of electronic components, for example) relocate in the low-density areas of the region—often bunching up with similar activities into "industrial parks," and usually setting up housing developments for employees. As our cities become less capable of absorbing higher population and activity densities, decentralization becomes the key word for new developments.

It is not really valid to continue to think about commuter movement in just the classical pattern. The ring/core pattern, of course, is, and will continue to be, dominant around most of our cities—at least those that developed large urban cores before the automobile came along. However, for the most part, Los Angeles is a post-automobile city/region, and its rush hour movement patterns appear a bit strange compared to those of other cities, since the work areas are not concentrated into one high-density urban core, but are scattered. The expressways fill with automobiles during rush hours, but in all directions, instead of just one-way as around the older cities. The great decentralization of work places and the generous expressway network has for many years postponed for Los Angeles the congestion problems of the radial-movement cities.

Los Angeles represents what is happening in the other RUEs. As the infilling between cities occurs, work/home relationships shift, leaving us unclear as to how we are to get a handle on the whole situation.

If we look at the Regional Urban Environment in terms of physical motion and land-use patterns, we can see that the environment is characterized by two distinctly different elements: (1) centralized activity areas; and (2) noncentralized activity areas.

(1) The centralized activity areas are those areas with significant numbers of people (or goods in specific instances) concentrated in a specific area for a significant length of time, such as shopping centers, schools, industrial areas, CBDs, high-

density apartment complexes, airports, government centers, stadia, and the like. Within a single town or city we are talking about hundreds of various activity "nodes"; in the Regional Urban Environment, about thousands of these nodes. We can also see that various nodes are active during times others are dormant, and vice versa, and that certain nodes involve great numbers of people, while others involve relatively few. The specific differences between the various nodes is beyond listing; the significant common characteristic is that these nodes require the admission of numbers of people (who must operate within the nodes as pedestrians), usually at fixed times, and the converse dispersal of these same people at later, usually fixed, times. There are some obvious exceptions to this timing arrangement, such as airports and retail shopping areas, where the people-loads are scattered a bit more randomly throughout the day and/or night, but they are the exceptions, not the rule, as the more predominant fixed-time activities generate the great peak movement activities of morning and evening. In our contemporary RUE these nodes are served by the automobile/roadway system. In most cases, the nodes must accommodate automobiles (up to as many as one per person) for the the duration of the activity-time per node. Another characteristic of the centralized activity area, or activity node, is the existence of occasional hierarchies of nodes, that is, large nodes can encompass several subnodes. For example, a CBD can contain a retail shopping area, a banking and finance area, a theater area, a hotel area, etc.; these subnodes in many instances being single buildings.

(2) The noncentralized activity areas of the RUE are basically represented by medium-to-low-density housing. While not exactly "activity spaces" per se, distinctly rural areas (that is, agricultural, wilderness, and park spaces) belong in this category, as they, like the suburban housing, fill the spaces

between the activity nodes in the region. As a general rule, the housing follows the conventional pattern of surrounding the cities; the farther from each city, the lower the density-level of the dwellings. However, most housing follows the existing access routes: the low-density housing spreads in linear patterns, following the highways, and linking up with the corresponding spread from adjacent cities. Sections of rural areas are either left untouched, as no significant roadways pass through those particular areas, or, patches or pockets of rural areas are surrounded by low-density housing areas. Of course, noncentralized activity spaces are not all to be found in the countryside. In some of the larger cities medium- and even high-density housing is extended over expansive geographical areas, too large to classify as nodes. We can look at the Regional Urban Environment, then, as a "field" of noncentralized activity areas upon which are scattered, seemingly at random, a large number of many-sized centralized activity areas (nodes). Since a large percentage of the noncentralized regional environment is devoted to housing—predominantly low density—we can see that transportation there is very widely dispersed, necking down to concentrated flow-forms at the centralized node areas. The most predominant flow pattern is that of motion from the noncentralized areas to the centralized areas in the mornings, and vice versa in the evenings, with many variations of this pattern at specific times (such as weekends, holidays, or special events such as ball games, etc.).

If we look at the region in these terms, we will see that the existing transportation setup, whether knowingly or not, is structured so that: (1) all activity nodes are interconnected, and (2) activity nodes and noncentralized areas are interconnected. For the most part, these tasks are delegated to the random-route system.

I contend that the random-route system is not adequate to

the task, and is in many ways inappropriate. Further, it is necessary to restructure the regional systems so that internodal commuter movements be conducted on fixed-route systems.

Peak commuter traffic is growing faster than the random-route system can handle it—the dramatically greater carrying capacity provided by fixed-route systems is the only solution to congestion problems in the case of the larger nodes. A secondary factor here is environmental: fixed-route systems can be buried without loss of capacity—the random route system cannot, and as the random-route system swells in size to meet motion demands, it covers over significant amounts of critically needed urban, suburban, and rural landspace, to say little of the blighting effect these roadways have on adjacent properties, or the economic impact of having great segments of land removed from tax rolls as they are paved under by public roadways.

To clarify my position, I'll outline a method of structuring a regional transportation system utilizing a more appropriate application of system types to meet the functional and environmental needs.

The first step would be to define just what geographical area is encompassed in a specific Regional Urban Environment. This requires little more than observation of established growth trends, a knowledge of how these regions develop, and a bit of "common sense."

Having established the region's approximate perimeters, every concentrated activity node within the region must be carefully defined and classified into a hierarchy, with those nodes attracting the greatest numbers of people and goods (such as city centers) at the top of the scale, the bottom of the scale being the very smallest nodes.

Once this first classification is made, the many relationships between the various sized nodes and between nodes and the noncentralized activity areas must be established. This would not actually be too difficult, since most of the relationships would be revealed in the process of determining the original activity nodes.

Let me point out that the identification and classification of activity nodes would have to be conducted by professional planners, sociologists, and politicians—the responsibility involved is quite large, since multitudes of judgments would have to be made, from a local to a regional level, regarding the desirability and undesirability of each of the specific nodes.

The next, and most obvious, step would be to organize a system of linking these elements together. This would be accomplished in the following manner:

(1) The major nodes (such as major city centers) would be linked first by direct non-stop high-speed rail systems.

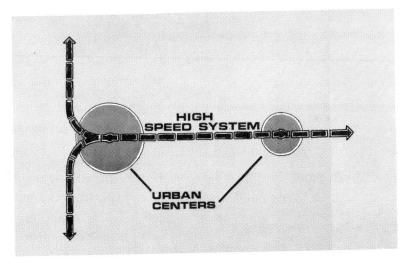

Figure 5-1.
High-speed fixed-route system. Drawing by Don Evans.

(2) A medium-speed system would form an extensive network throughout the whole region, interconnecting every significant activity node, including those aforementioned major ones.

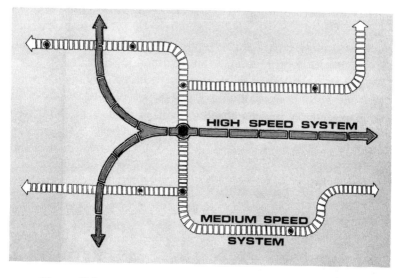

Figure 5-2.
Medium-speed fixed-route system. Drawing by Don Evans.

(3) Most of the nodes served by the medium-speed system represent the interface between the centralized and noncentralized portions of the region, as they, for the most part, would be located in suburban residential areas. From these nodes low-speed "collection" systems, such as small buses or minitrains, could operate, shuttling people from their homes to the node-station.

The most significant aspect of this proposal is the scale of the medium-speed layout involved. This would not only link nodes within the high-density urban areas, such as in the older cities, but would encompass the many scattered nodes formed in the medium-to-low-density areas surrounding the urban cores, and in the landspaces between urban cores, such as shopping cen-

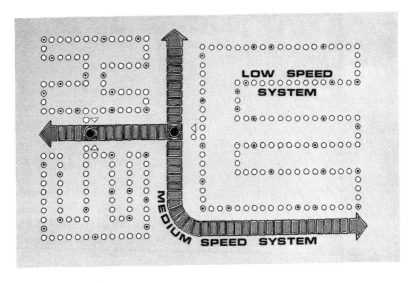

Figure 5-3.
Low-speed (collection) fixed-route system. Drawing by Don Evans.

ters, industrial parks, air terminals, and other such centralized activities in generally noncentralized landscape.

The intent of the medium-speed layout is to make all the significant activity nodes within a region mutually accessible by fixed-route transport. The random-route system made possible the great horizontal medium-to-low-density spread (which the early fixed-route systems were never designed to serve), but is now failing to accommodate commuter movements between these areas and the high-density urban centers. I am proposing a *comprehensive* medium-speed fixed-route commuter movement system, responsive to regional transportation requirements.

One of the newest and largest medium-speed, fixed-route commuter movement systems, the San Francisco Bay Area Rapid Transit, recognizes, in part, that the Bay Region extends beyond the limits of the city of San Francisco, yet it fails to meet the test of comprehensiveness, as demonstrated by two consultants for the project, Tallie B. Maule and John E. Burchard:

> BARTD is not an integrated metropolitan transportation system. It is more nearly a high-speed, luxurious interurban and commuter service extending well into the country. It is capable of some local use in the downtown areas but it does not provide really convenient access to most of the important points in San Francisco whether Union Square, North Beach, the Japanese Trade Center, the parks, the Opera House, Candlestick Park, the Cow Palace, or the Airport; over in the East Bay its relations to the main things in Oakland is but a little better while the walk to any central point on the Berkeley campus of the University of California will be long and tiring and all uphill. If BARTD does become a transportation success it will be because somebody else has provided all the feeder lines, separately owned, separately managed, and jealously so; it will be because private motor cars have played a major role in delivering commuters to outlying stations as a sort of revival of the old song about the 5:15. The people of the Bay Area never really discussed whether what they actually wanted was an integrated transportation system, and they went out of their way in the BARTD charter to be sure that the BARTD directors and management did not indulge in any illegitimate aspirations of that sort.

This decision, or non-decision, has of course been a major conditioner of design. It was not a decision made by the management or the Board of BARTD. It is hard to believe that they might have stretched the powers of their charter far enough to have made any difference. We do not know how hard they tried to get a broader charter; perhaps not very hard. But even if they had, one could not be sanguine of their success, given the abrasive and divisive nature of the local rivalries. The fact is that American metropolises need integrated systems right now; that systems engineers are almost certainly about to design them now. We know of no system yet in advanced planning in the United States that promises this or which goes much further than to think in interurban, suburban, or simply downtown terms. This is, of course, more complicated than the need for single ownership and management. It is an indispensable condition but it is not sufficient. It will then require imagination and money and an ability to deal with the many who regard the American automobile as their only true castle, superior to those of the Middle Ages in that it is their privilege to move it anywhere, any time, and be guaranteed a place to put it on arrival. BARTD will be something which many people of the Bay Area can use and enjoy and something of which they can be proud, but it will not serve the metropolitan area in the way the networks of the Paris Metro and the London Underground do.[1]

A system that fails to acknowledge significant activity nodes within its territorial range is not comprehensive. BARTD is admittedly skeletal . . . but it is a start. The system that more nearly represents what I mean by comprehensive service is the Metro of Washington, D.C. This system is metropolitan, rather

1. Tallie B. Maule and John E. Burchard, "Design Procedures for the Bay Area," *Journal of the Franklin Institute* 286 (November 1968): 433–34. Reprinted by permission of the *Journal of the Franklin Institute*.

than regional, in scope, but offers the best coverage of the suburban ring to be found with any of the ring/core cities, as it links over forty suburban nodes with the D.C. core.

The Metro example is instructive also in approaching the question regarding the continued utility of existing bus transit systems. In this case, operation of the bus system will fall under the control of the Metro authority (upon completion of rail construction), and the buses will be assigned low-speed suburban collection roles (serving the suburban stations), as well as continuing as a medium-speed transit system, operating in the many gaps left by the initial Metro layout. In fact, Metro planners anticipate that 70 percent of the rail passengers will have a bus ride on one end of each trip. This, incidentally, is characteristic of Montreal's Metro system, where the suburban rail stations are served by localized bus routes.

A more profound question, at this point, than the integration of existing bus systems into a regional railed commuter-movement system is the continued role of the random-route system.

A generally common characteristic of commuter movements is that they involve a low-density, noncentralized environment on one end, and a higher density activity node on the other. The random-route system operates most effectively in the former environment, the fixed-route system in the latter. When the random-route system plays the role of both collecting from a low-density area and delivering to a high-density area, it develops the familiar congestion and parking problems in the latter area. On the other hand, the fixed-route system is poorly structured to handle the collecting role in noncentralized areas . . . while it operates quite efficiently in high-density areas.

It should be obvious that a medium-speed system, if laid out on a comprehensive regional scale, would, in a great many instances, link together widely spaced nodes in low-density areas. The random-route system would be the only practical home-to-station movement means in most of these cases. The regions will absorb most of the population growth between now and the turn of the century, and a significant amount of this growth will be accommodated in low- to medium-density housing in the undeveloped landspaces between and around the cities that define the region; thus, the automobile will have a definite continued commuter role.

Regarding commuter movements, I am proposing a complementary system. To assure that it is complementary and not two competitive systems, precise commuter roles must be assigned to both the fixed-route and random-route systems. For example, if we construct a fixed-route network to carry commuter loads, and the random-route system is allowed to continue carrying these same loads, many of the purposes for transferring these loads to fixed-route systems to begin with are lost, and the two systems are placed in competition for public funds. This, of course, is what has happened in all cities . . . with fixed-route systems receiving the short end of the stick.

For the commuter movement proposal to function as outlined, activity nodes that attract great numbers of commuters must simply be placed "off limits" to automobiles during commuter hours. Since the private automobile places tremendous burdens on the city center, it represents a luxury item, as the individual involved is the only beneficiary of the automobile's presence there—leading logically enough to the conclusion that, as with all luxuries, the individual should have to bear the economic burden. Placing an exorbitantly high entry toll rate around the high-density activity nodes during commuter hours, high enough to be prohibitive for the daily commuter, would both force the commuter to seek public transport and still allow access for those willing to pay the price—and, incidentally, the toll revenue could be channeled back into the total transportation system. Obviously, the fixed-route network must be in place prior to restricting commuter movements on the random-route system, but the latter must follow rapidly.

What happens, then, regarding noncommuter movements? Would the establishment of the proposed commuter-movement network, with its restrictions on random-route commuter movements, have implications for the noncommuter use of the automobile?

The automobile represents the greatest achievement of personal mobility known to man. I mean this, of course, in the sense of mass accessibility—the average American is not likely to have an Apollo lunar module in his driveway, but he is likely to have a Chevy, a Ford, or a VW. The freedom of mobility that has been available to us in this century is unparalleled . . . and not easy to relinquish. Of course, this freedom is being progressively limited by the functional limitations of the random-route system, but we tend to preserve the illusion that everything will work out—and to view proposals for fixed-route systems as threats, instead of as preservers of mobility. Functional limitations of the random-route system will force the introduction of a certain amount of fixed-route systems (whether by my plan or not), and in each case the effort will threaten the dominance of the random-route system, as public funds are not infinite, and we are not really in a position to conduct an ambitious construction program of fixed-route systems while sustaining expressway construction programs at the same pace: the latter must yield.

However, if we place most regional commuter movements on a regional system as outlined, the maximum commuter role of the automobile would be as a shuttle between home and neighborhood station. As suburban densities rise (as they will), neighborhood-scale fixed-route collector systems (shuttle buses and minitrains) become practical in many areas, minimizing the role of the automobile as a commuter device in those areas. By the very fact that the node-to-node rail network would link all commercial activity centers, it would attract a significant amount of noncommuter movement, such as shopping trips. Also, recreation and entertainment-oriented movements could occur to a great extent on the fixed-route system, since it would (if designed properly) tie in such nodes as stadia, amusement parks, civic auditoria, etc. (The current traffic load for these activities, especially on weekends, is almost alarming, and must be recognized.) Should we establish a comprehensive commuter system, one that links together most significant activity spots in the region, we might well see a decline in the automobile population growth rate, since the individual would be able to conduct a significant amount of his movement activities without it.

This proposal is, simply enough, an advocation of a massive investment in railed transit systems (in the various RUEs) . . . an investment to the same degree we presently make in the random-route system. The proposal is a schematic outline of a long-range transportation policy . . . a very expensive policy, and one obviously difficult to instigate, as it would clearly work against the random-route system's industrial and governmental "establishment." It would also meet resistance by an automobile-loving public, who would recognize that following such a policy would put a halt to the continuous spread of asphalt . . . which would dramatically hamper the flow patterns of the growing automobile population.

So why bother with such a complex, expensive, and probably unpopular scheme? The functional and environmental problems associated with our contemporary transportation methods, compounded by the phenomenal population growth rate, are already forcing us to seek alternate solutions. Our best course of action is to plot a scheme that provides the most appropriate response to the many problems that face us today, but on a scale that anticipates tomorrow's movement and land-use requirements. To do this, we must think in comprehensive regional terms, even though we are not yet able to act on this level, or we risk implementing immediate solutions that do not face the long-range problems.

Even so, why think of an extended fixed-route system as being the valid solution? The functional limitations of the random-route system in terms of commuter movement congestion and parking requirements in high-density activity areas are already enough to force the discussion of fixed-route alternates in most United States cities of significant size. However, the feasibility of installing railed transit systems is questionable in many instances, and the concept of placing most of the commuter movements within a Regional Urban Environment seems, at first glance, quite implausible.

Conventional transit economics maintain that a surface rail system must haul around 5,000 passengers a day, and a subsurface system around 40,000 a day, to be operable . . . which means a lower limit of one million population to support a railed transit system. However, these figures are formulated in the context of today's transportation scene.

The existing railed transit systems carry only a tiny fraction of this country's daily commuter movements, and only receive a tiny percentage of our overall transportation subsidies. Most of the existing systems provide only limited service in terms of comprehensive routing and comfort. They are "second choice" systems in the public eye and desirable only when congestion and parking limitations, products of high population concentrations, make them the only transportation choice.

Vastly extending railed transit routing so that it realistically serves the suburban areas within the region—placing the service in the laps of the customers, so to speak; capitalizing on technological advances, such as lightweight vehicle construction and computerized flow control; and reinvesting a great bulk of the transportation subsidy monies from expressway construction to railed transit construction would make present day rules-of-thumb invalid . . . a whole new transportation economics picture would be formed.

Is it feasible, functionally or economically, to sustain our commitment to the random-route system when functional and environmental conditions make the fixed-route system more appropriate for commuter movement needs? Turn of the century planners would have been overwhelmed had they known the size of the random-route system we find essential for today's movement needs . . . hopefully, we can accurately anticipate the needs of the coming century, and not choke on the realization that it will require a significant break from our present way of doing things.

Six

LAND-USE IMPLICATIONS

THE FUNCTIONAL LIMITATIONS of the random-route system in handling commuter movements are forcing us to seek alternate methods. However, an alternate that satisfies the functional requirements without responding appropriately to environmental conditions is no longer good enough.

A strong case can be made for a proposal to place a majority of commuter movements on rail for the reason that a rail system can be buried where desired, to avoid the blighting associated with urban expressways, as well as move people in and out of high-density areas without imposing automobile parking demands on those areas. These are by no means small considerations. It is essential that we call a halt to the continued prostration of our living and working landspaces to the demands of the random-route system, and the growing community resistance to urban expressway construction should demonstrate that our tolerance for such practices is rapidly lowering.

However, this is not enough. If we consider the introduction of a new movement system, we must examine its implications in the context of large scale land-use patterns and trends.

The large-scale land use phenomena of consequence (today, and in the foreseeable future) is the formation and maturation of a series of Regional Urban Environments, as discussed in chapter 4. Actually, this is not an easily recognized phenomena in many areas, as land-use changes underway are more commonly identified as "sprawl," "decentralization," "redistribution," or "scatterization." The issue is further confused when related to the apparent differences between the ring/core (with high-density core) East Coast cities and the medium-to-low-density "sprawl" cities of the West Coast.

In city-scale terms, the buildup of the region is most easily seen as decentralization, as much of the new population growth is being accommodated in low-density housing and working areas developing at ever greater distances from city cores. The growing density (meanwhile) of the city cores, producing increased circulation problems, encourages the "scatterization" of all kinds of activities into the low-density outlying areas.

On a larger scale, however, such decentralization can be seen as infilling. That is, the low-density outlying areas are in reality the undeveloped spaces between cities, and the decentralization activity is in effect filling in the gaps between the cities, thus defining the regions. At this point, with the older East Coast cities, the development is still radial in nature; the growth still quite obviously radiates outward from distinct high-density points. With the newer cities of the West Coast (and elsewhere), where large, preautomobile urban cores did not develop, the region-formation is not so much a decentralization from large cores, but instead low-density infilling between many low-density cores. The Los Angeles basin, for example, was at one time many small distinct communities, but they have long been assimilated into a region . . . and this region is becoming part of a larger RUE stretching down the coast from San Francisco past Los Angeles to San Diego.

There are really no profound differences between the coastal land-use development trends, except that the West Coast examples are in a more advanced state, as they were formed almost from their beginnings by the random-route system, whereas the preautomobile structures of the Eastern cities have been able to absorb enough of the population growth to postpone the horizontal development.

As outlined in chapter 4, there are problem areas common to RUE developments. As the RUEs absorb the growing population, activity nodes spring up in multitudes of locations, not in accordance with a master regional plan of any sort, a situation which becomes meaningful when we realize that a significant portion of the regional landspace must be preserved for agricultural and recreational activities. Also, when an area becomes saturated with low-to-medium-density developments (such as the Los Angeles basin), and the population continues to grow, higher density nodes will develop, whether in desired locations or not.

The point is that we have no region-scaled controls to assure that the RUE growth phenomena will appropriately meet the needs of the growing population, in terms of providing environmental choices to accommodate a variety of life styles. Jean Gottman, in his essay "Urban Sprawl and Its Ramifications," suggests that our concerns should now be: the possibility of preserving or establishing the "small-town" environment within Megalopolis (such as is attempted in the new-town concepts); managing the blend between the desired features of the urban life and the desired features of the suburban/semirural life, as found throughout the region; and establishing control over the "sprawl" situation.[2]

We might never develop direct region-wide land-use controls, as the complexity of consolidating the multitudes of existing governmental units involved might well prove prohibitive.

2. Jean Gottman, "Urban Sprawl and Its Ramifications," *Metropolis on the Move* (New York: John Wiley & Sons, Inc., 1967), p. 3.

However, transportation systems are often controlled on a state- or region-sized scale. As it is my contention that transportation methods have much to say about land uses, I see region-wide control over transportation as a means of establishing a certain amount of region-wide control over land uses. More specifically, I see a node-to-node regional rail system, as proposed, as an active regional land-use planning tool.

The proposed movement system would act as a matrix, or framework, for pinpointing the geographical locations of density buildups. By specifying station locations throughout the region, we designate focal points for activities in each area. By dictating the basic movement patterns (commuter movements) in an area, we dictate, to a great extent, land uses.

For example, node stations located in noncentralized areas would play the key "interface" role between random-route and fixed-route motion, thus exerting a certain amount of environmental influence. The placement of a rail station in a suburban location, a station linking that spot with the work activity nodes that the residents of that area must travel to on a regular basis, obviously focuses a great deal of physical activity on that spot. By acting as an accumulator for the area it serves, the node station will have a land-use effect on the environment—primarily due to the fact it is a natural market area for many commercial amenities, acting as a mini-shopping center, in a sense.

If we structure the commuter-movement setup so that the only realistic choice the suburbanite has is transport at the local station, we have made that station a significant part of that individual's daily life patterns. We are, in effect, dictating that a great accumulation of suburban commuters gather at a selected point twice daily. Since this activity point is a natural developer of commercial activity, it seems logical to relate station positioning with the existing and/or desired commercial land uses in the area.

Sometimes an appropriate nodal activity will occur within a noncentralized activity area, such as a shopping center within a surrounding suburban housing area, for a transportation collection-point. This is ideal for this purpose, since the shopping center, made part of a system linking it to the other nodes in the region, would benefit from the daily shopping movement

Figures 6-1, 6-2, 6-3, 6-4, 6-5.
The BART and Metro systems layouts have included significant probes into low-density suburbia. These suburban stations have been planned to be surrounded by parking. However, as land values rise around the stations, parking lots will yield to other activities, with the parking accommodated in buildings, or alleviated by the services of neighborhood collector buses. Courtesy Bay Area Rapid Transit District and Washington Metropolitan Area Transit Authority.

patterns throughout the system (as opposed to a center excluded from the system, and therefore cut off from accessibility for other than just neighborhood customers).

Also, the shopping center is an ideal neighborhood collection-point as it provides shopping, entertainment, and other amenities for the commuter on his way to, or on his way from, his

place of work. Again, focusing the daily activity patterns of a large number of residents through a common point, such as this center, could only boost the size and scope of amenities available in the center. Over a period of time, what was formerly just a shopping center would become a true neighborhood center due to its position in the daily life-patterns of the residents involved.

Often, however, a residential area will not have an appropriate node established. At this point, the proposed system takes on a positive, active role. The location of a collection-point (station) in a node-less area, that station being linked by medium-speed rail to the overall system, would create in that locale, over a period of time, the same type of neighborhood center as described before: large numbers of people passing through a specific location on a regular basis attracts like a magnet the appropriate commercial activities.

It should now be possible to think of this railed system as a tool for planning regional land use. If we control movement patterns within a geographical area, we control, to a large extent, the use of the land-space in that area. If we can create neighborhood centers by this method, it follows that we can create whole neighborhoods. It should be obvious that an accessibility point (a station), on an established rail system, deliberately located in a formerly undeveloped area would positively contribute to the development of that area. Of course, many factors would determine the actual nature of the development of that area, but certain movement patterns would already be established, patterns focused on a central point, making that point a potential neighborhood activity-core for the development.

We already have experience in introducing a fixed-route commuter-movement system into an existing urban scene . . . the station nodes acting as focal points for development . . . as evidenced in Toronto and San Francisco. G. Warren Heenan, one of Canada's top real estate appraisers, in discussing the impact of the rail transit system in Toronto, says: "If an urban rapid transit system never earned a dime, it would still pay for itself a thousand times over through its beneficial impact on real estate values and increased assessments." The Yonge Street subway cost $67 million, and ignited a $10 billion development explosion along the line.[3] James E. Clayton, editorial staff member of the *Washington Post*, reports on the BART system in San Francisco:

> Within walking distance of BART's six central stations in the downtown areas of San Francisco, Oakland, and Berkeley, private investment in new office buildings since BART was authorized in 1962 is now approaching a billion dollars. Part of this, according to one of the city's best real estate experts, would have come without the construction of the rapid transit system but some of it would not, at least not in these particular locations.

He considers the BART example an object lesson regarding the long-range impact of a railed system on an urban area, as property values near stations went up in every case, in many cases doubling. BART is being used as an urban redevelopment tool on Market Street, it is prompting the construction of the

3. G. Warren Heenan, "Rapid Transit and Property Value," *Community Planning Review*, Spring 1967, pp. 6–7.

first major buildings in downtown Berkeley in forty years, and is forcing many Bay communities to consider the BART stations as nuclei for new commercial or high-density residential developments. Clayton finds only two faults: the communities involved did not fully realize the scope of impact and the potentials involved, and shrewd developers who did recognize

the situation carried away as profit much of the $1.3 billion system cost: "If the government bought such land at the pre-improvement value and sold it after the appreciation occurred, the profit would go a long way toward paying for the improvements." [4]

Structuring a transportation matrix allows us, incidentally, to

4. James E. Clayton, "Developing the Opportunities in Rapid Transit," *The Washington Post*, February 2, 1970, p. A13.

play a significant social role, as demonstrated in the planning of Seattle's fixed-route system. That city's former mayor, J. D. Bramen, is credited for the inclusion (over patronage-conscious and cost-minded resistance) of an otherwise excluded low-income enclave (the "Central Area") into that system, by designating that area for a station location.[5] This is no small point, as low-income ghettos in most cities could be aided significantly by making the outside world (distant jobs, entertainment, and recreation areas) more accessible for their inhabitants.

The other side of the coin is land-use control by access denial. Placing station nodes in specific locations obviously precludes their placement in other locations. Planner Roger Starr comments on this condition with reference to the commuter fixed-route systems serving New York City:

> The rapid transit lines fanning out from the city center have unquestionably helped the city to add new landspace by minimizing the cost in time of putting it to use each morning; a close look at the pattern of development, however, reveals that the buildings and the homes did not develop equally along the new mass transit lines. The development, rather, consisted of a series of rings, each centered around a single rapid transit station. The land lying further away from the stations, or between them, was not developed until later; its development could not be achieved until a local street pattern became real and not merely a fiction on a map, and until the local street pattern was connected to the major attractions of the city by a respectable highway network.[6]

With due respect to Mr. Starr, this aspect of developing via

5. "Transit's Power to Shape a Region," *Architectural Forum,* January–February 1968, p. 57.
6. Roger Starr, *Urban Choices: The City and Its Critics* (Baltimore: Penguin Books, Inc., 1966), p. 192.

fixed-route transportation can be very advantageous to us when we desire to preserve landspace for agricultural or recreational purposes, or when we simply wish to provide buffer landspace between developments.

If we desire continuous land development, we need only to place stations in close sequence; if not, we spread them out, and

deliberately fail to provide Mr. Starr's "respectable highway network." Station spacing on a line can also play a role regarding the commercial strip phenomena: for the same reason that distant station spacing breaks up Mr. Starr's housing developments, strategic station spacing could prevent the development of new strips, and cause the dissolution of existing strips, should we wish such things.

In the face of the development of the RUEs, what do we want from our transportation methods? Obviously we want comprehensive movement service, by any means. However, is this all?

I contend that committing our regional commuter movements to fixed-route systems as proposed could offer us some significant options in regional land-use control. Positive and negative access control (access to specific areas by a commuter-movement system) would mean control over the geographic location of commuter-related activity nodes. We can use transportation as an active land-use planning tool; by committing our regional commuter movements to rail, we can assure that we can accommodate our booming population in an orderly fashion and we can assure the development of the RUE's as comprehensive entities, not as chaotic growths.

On one hand I must stress the urgency for transferring regional commuter movements to fixed-route systems, not only to rescue us from worsening congestion problems, but also to spare us the environmental damage caused by the continuous expansion of the regional roadway network, which grows and grows as congestion problems grow. I am convinced that we must act quickly to prevent expressway construction from making great segments of the urban and suburban environment simply unfit for human habitation. Do not forget that there is a huge economic and governmental machine geared to do one thing: build roadways . . . and it will do that with much enthusiasm until such time that we reprogram it for different tasks. While we agonize over our problems, this machine, in the name of solving them, is compounding them.

On the other hand, I must insert a word of caution: we cannot let our actions outpace policy-making. Dashing hither and yon establishing fixed-route systems to resolve localized random-route congestion problems, in the manner of chasing down and extinguishing brush fires, does not represent a valid planning philosophy, although it is the manner of transportation planning to which we are most accustomed. We will not have demonstrated much foresight if at some time we find a region served by several localized fixed-route commuter systems, each designed as an entity, each incompatible with the other (not just in equipment types, but also in basic layout philosophies) —making it difficult if not impossible to form a comprehensive total system for the region.

The only responsible method of handling our future transportation situation is to recognize the functional and environmental characteristics of the system types available, determine what we wish the environmental land-use scheme to be, and structure the transportation systems accordingly. In short, we must recognize that transportation planning is, to a significant extent, land-use planning. Transportation is a planning tool, which means that we must not only know how the tool works, we also must know what we want to do with it. Only by determining overall goals, and formulating policy-strategies (such as outlining a regional commuter movement network), can we be in a position of *acting* instead of *reacting*.

Seven

TRANSPORTATION AND MAN

Commuter trains and buses would reduce a city's traffic problems—but only if the suburbanite could see that taking a train is cheaper and more convenient and more comfortable than driving to town. There is a man in Connecticut, for example, who drives to his New York City job each day. He knows he averages 20 miles an hour in the rush hour traffic in the best of times. He knows the train averages 14 miles an hour faster. He knows it would be cheaper to take the train, because his automobile costs him nearly 12¢ a mile to own and use. Yet, he drives it to work. Why?

"Mainly," he said, "I don't like public transportation. If there's going to be any transportation, let's have it private. Besides, my car is a lot more comfortable than any seat on that square-wheeled train."

So, he comes to the office badly in need of coffee, jittery and irritable from his matutinal bout with the traffic, but still thinking he's been more comfortable in his car than he would have been in the train. He thinks that driving his car means he's not part of a public transportation system, when in fact the sole difference between himself and a train rider is that the one is fighting traffic every inch of the way while the other spends the same miles reading the paper. Otherwise,

neither has real privacy or freedom of action. Both
are sitting in New York-bound machines, with other sitters
in the endless line before and behind them.[1]

THE MOST NATURAL COURSE of a dialogue involving two diverse
forms of transportation, when overall transportation problems
are pending, is to choose one form over the other, and demonstrate in melodramatic fashion how one form is irrevocably bad
and the other unquestionably superior. It is tempting to casti-
gate the random-route system and place the fixed-route system
on a pedestal, for various reasons. J. B. Jackson, in the Spring
1968 issue of *Landscape*, counters this trend of thinking with
these observations:

> The planners' dislike for accelerating American dependence
> on the automobile is a major determinant of much contem-
> porary urban design. Unrestricted use of the private car does
> have its disadvantages. It causes pollution. It is a markedly
> inefficient method of peak load transportation to and from the
> crowded centers of our cities. It demands heavy expenditures
> for the two car commuter family. It magnifies the already
> difficult problem of preserving wilderness areas. Most seri-
> ously of all, it is producing a new city shape which the plan-
> ning profession, educated in traditional concepts of urban
> physical structure, has so far been unable to cope with.
>
> But the anti-automobile bias of the professionals seems to
> be based upon more than such rational objections. Putting
> aside supercilious descriptions of the American's car as a
> lover-image or a totem, the fact remains that the automobile
> does have a meaning that for many people reaches far beyond
> its function—an emotional attachment represented by the
> weekend rituals of washing or tinkering. It might be just this

1. John Keats, *The Insolent Chariots* (Greenwich, Conn.: Fawcett Publica-
tions, Inc., 1964), p. 162.

attachment, as much as its functional limitations, that explains the low esteem in which the automobile is held by planners. Somehow strolling the streets, sipping wine at a sidewalk cafe, playing chess in the park, sampling the art galleries or gathering for darts at a pub are all considered worthwhile pastimes for the urban dweller, while repairing or grooming cars is somehow distasteful. This is a distinction that smacks at bottom of class-consciousness or snobbery. It is a reflection of the profession's unspoken vision of the city as primarily a stimulating setting for the urbane connoisseur.

But far more dangerous than the planners' emotional aversion to the automobile is their total failure to understand the reasons for its popularity. The kind of pseudo-Freudian analysis popularized by John Keats and others is more useful in justifying existing prejudices than in furthering real understanding. And yet in the collection of contemporary planning concepts there exists a powerful and obvious tool for the understanding of the automobile's role—the concept of territoriality.

There is, to be sure, more than a bit of gobbledygook and silliness and plain misunderstanding in the designers' current preoccupation with some of the newer concepts of the psychology of spatial perception. But the work of Hall and others has shown, plainly and surely, that men move through, build around them, and carry about with them, certain structured volumes of psychologically differentiated space. There is doubt as to how these spatial volumes are best understood, and doubt as to their existence or their—at least sometimes—importance. Nor should there be doubt that constriction or expansion of these distinct spaces, or conflicts between them, or ambiguities as to their boundaries, can cause uncertainty and stress.

This idea of man as living within a range of simultaneous spatial domains graded from the intimately personal to the plainly public, should explain, more satisfactorily than any of the many familiar psychiatric or sociological cliches, the attraction of the automobile. Put simply, the automobile allows one to travel almost at will anywhere in the public domain while remaining in a completely private world unequivocally defined by physical boundaries. The maintenance, defense or even definition of this intensely personal space no longer needs to be achieved by psychological adaptation or cultural understanding or ritual. It is marked off structurally —with clarity and solidity. Perhaps Americans are more concerned than most peoples with the definition of personal space —though Hall claims that the Germans are even more jealous of its boundaries. It might be that the rapid and continuing changes in the American social scene over the last fifty years have produced a general uncertainty and unease that places more importance and value upon the protection and clear definition of the private personal realm. While the traditional Utopian visions have been built around a communal structure, modern Americans are attempting to build very personal or at least familial Utopias—Utopias structured around detached houses, television and automobiles. There is at any rate a basic distinction between the automobile and other methods of transportation that far transcends convenience and economy, a distinction that must be understood. It is the distinction between *public* and *private* transportation, not in the sense of financing or titular ownership or even trip scheduling, but in the sense of the *personal perception of space patterns*.

This ability to move through public space without suffering impingements upon, or readjustment of, one's own personal space, could explain much more than the commuter's attachment to his private automobile. It might partly explain the phenomenal success of the auto rental companies, for a rental car allows one to travel a strange and foreign and often confusing public world in a kind of instant privacy and encapsulated security. It might partly explain, as much as laziness, the propensity for taking automobiles into the "wilderness" areas—areas that by definition lie at the opposite extreme from personalized space. Surely it explains much of the success of the motel business, for a motel is more than just convenient—it enables one to move between the personal spaces of car and bedroom, without traveling through the more public and often spatially ambiguous realms of lobby, elevator and corridor associated with the traditional hotel.

It must be understood that the automobile is not just a more or less efficient competitor of public transit, nor must the emotional importance of the automobile be contemptuously dismissed as some psychological aberration. It might be that in certain parts of our older cities the side effects of the private automobile are so space and time consuming, so physically wasteful or even unhealthy as to require restrictions on its use. It might be, too, that the only way of increasing the acceptance of "public" transportation is to incorporate into it as much of spatial quality of the automobile as is possible. But the transportation problems of our urban regions are not going to be solved until we admit to an understanding of the very special spatial features of the automobile, for it is likely that the appeal of the automobile is not just a silly habit easily gotten rid of, but a means of fulfilling deeply rooted concepts of human territoriality.[2]

Responsible transportation planning will not result from a cat-fight between random-route and fixed-route proponents. Each system possesses its own set of operational and environmental characteristics—the trick is to preserve the best features of each system, eliminate the undesirable ones, in a way that not only resolves the immediate problems, but is responsible for the land-use and circulation situations of the future.

The complexity of this situation must be appreciated. We cannot agree on the best solutions to our immediate functional problems. We cannot agree on what effects transportation methods have on the environment, and we cannot agree on

2. J. B. Jackson, *Landscape* 17 (Spring 1968): 2.

what we want from the environment. This situation is compounded by the fact that solving our immediate functional problems and resolving future transportation/land-use relationships could even prove mutually exclusive.

Without established long-range transportation/land-use planning goals, we are forced, by default, into following reactionary transportation planning policies—the functional problems will not wait. Resolution of the immediate problems could take several forms, but unless we know what we want for the future, we cannot make a responsible choice of methods. I am not saying that transportation methods are the only land-use form-determinants, but I do maintain that they play a very significant role—and we cannot afford to be complacent about what methods we use.

So, what do we want? If we concede that both random-route and fixed-route systems are here to stay, we can ask that the quality of experiences of the passengers be equally good for each. As it now stands, the random-route system has the lead in four important areas: (1) privacy, (2) comfort, (3) orientation, and (4) convenience.

(1) *Privacy.* The great mix of economic and ethnic backgrounds represented in regional commuter movements is made tolerable for many people by the physical isolation that their automobiles allow them—there is no physical or social contact with those in other vehicles. The ability to select one's fellow passengers is an option within the random-route system that should not be underrated.

(2) *Comfort.* The automobile offers many amenities for personal comfort, limited only by one's ability to pay for them. These generally include adjustable seats, individual temperature controls, radio, etc. One can seal himself off from contact with the world outside the vehicle, and be entertained to boot.

Significantly, each automobile rider has a seat: none is forced to stand.

(3) *Orientation.* The automobile-user, due to the fact that he must navigate his vehicle, rarely has disorientation problems, as he has a continuing awareness of his routing and the distance to his destination.

(4) *Convenience.* The random-route system approximates a door-to-door transport system, as the suburbanite always has his vehicle parked at hand, and can drive to his job without having to transfer vehicles. Of course, when he works in a high-density city-center, his chances of parking near his job are becoming increasingly slim but for those who both live and work in low-density areas, this is the optimum system.

The fixed-route system needs consideration in these same categories:

PRIVACY

Two kinds of privacy are relevant to a discussion of the design of public transport systems. One is *physical* privacy; the other is *cultural* privacy. By the term physical privacy we refer to the need of human beings to be separated spatially from each other. The actual distance which one person wants to be removed from another varies relative to the situation in which both are involved and the social characteristics of each. The norms for public transport are interesting because the relations among passengers are such that they ought to be far removed from each other—say, at a distance the customer is from the salesperson—when, in fact, the exigencies of public transport often force them into unnecessary physical contact. Particularly on longer rides, or when vehicles are crowded, the stress induced by unavoidably close proximity often exceeds the capacity of the rider to cope with it, and a feeling of discomfort develops which contributes to the general aversion for public transport.

Cultural privacy refers to the need and desire of individuals to be among other persons who share their values, norms, beliefs, and standards of behavior, and to exclude from their presence individuals with other norms and standards. We see expression of this need and desire in all the rules established for membership in groups, in the ways in which people attempt to restrict the entry of newcomers or strangers to social gatherings, professions, neighborhoods, decision-making groups, and the like. In public transport environments it is obviously difficult for passengers to establish any kind of cultural privacy for the simple reason that subways and urban bus systems are accessible to all those who have the small amount of money required for fare. The ambition of passengers to transform them into hospitable settings for homogeneous groups, however, can often be observed. The leaders of a group of travelers will rush ahead into the car or bus and try to take over a section of seats so that they and their friends following can occupy them together. Passengers have an easier time exerting this kind of control on commuter trains which are less densely packed and which attract the same people daily.

It is interesting to note about these efforts to humanize the transport environment and make it into a situation where groups can form and interaction take place that they have no legal support in the laws regulating public carriers or in the administrative rules of the transport authorities. Indeed, there is some question whether they are sanctioned even by the informal norm structure of the society. For example, it is never clear whether, in a crowded train, a passenger should be allowed to hold a seat for a friend who is boarding late; or whether a passenger should move to another seat to accommodate two friends who accidentally meet. In general, the norms are more supportive of the right to demand cultural privacy on commuter trains than on buses or subways, where the idea of equal rights for all passengers unquestionably prevails.[3]

There is no simple method of aligning physical vehicle environments with these complex sociological needs. We find individual privacy requirements at odds with potential carrying capacities: quality versus quantity. The achievement of physical and/or cultural privacy is made doubly difficult where standing and seated passengers mix in the same car, as the obvious inequities create unavoidable tensions on long trips. By standing the passengers, the vehicle capacity can be boosted, which, as the following chart indicates, is the standard procedure, as great passenger demands are made on limited systems. The evidence suggests that 100 percent seating and a large amount of floor space per person (6 to 8 square feet) is most desirable from the privacy standpoint in a conventional type car.

Compartmented transit cars, with various sized compartments, all with exterior doors, could offer the maximum of privacy, assuming that one were placed in a compartment with acceptable fellow travelers. This assumption could trip us up, and for this reason I lean toward a system that could carry many vehicle configurations, at least for the middle-speed element of the system, since this would allow the linking together into trains of various styles of vehicle configurations, allowing experimentation in favoring passenger preferences.

Our present railed transit systems, for the most part, are all too crowded, and the systems too small, to allow the low passenger-per-car densities that our privacy requirements demand. The only solution to this is to construct the regional

3. Robert Gutman, "Urban Transporters and Human Environments," *Journal of the Franklin Institute* 286 (November 1968): 534. Reprinted by permission of the *Journal of the Franklin Institute*.

system on a scale that could handle movement demands without stretching the capacity of each vehicle, as we do now.

A possible method of assuring a certain amount of cultural privacy on the system would be to introduce an economic-class segregation by establishing a dual fare system, possibly

STATISTICS ON EXISTING FIXED-ROUTE SYSTEM VEHICLES [4]

Vehicle Type	Approx. Car Length	Passenger Capacity			Space per Passenger
		Total	Seated	% Seated	
Westinghouse Transit Expressway	31 ft.	70	28	40%	4.0 sq. ft.
Typical Motor Bus	40	75	53	71%	4.3
Chicago	48	183	47	26%	2.3
Cleveland	49	196	54	22%	2.3
New York IRT	51	200	44	22%	2.3
Philadelphia	55	202	56	28%	2.5
Milan	58	213	26	12%	2.4
New York BMT-IRT	61	300	50	17%	2.0
Moscow	62	250	44	18%	2.2
Boston (Camb.-Ash)	70	307	56	18%	2.3
SFBARTD	70	144	72	50%	4.8
Toronto (Bloor)	74	338	84	25%	1.7
Washington	75	161	82	51%	4.6
Long Island C.C.	85	124	124	100%	6.8

along the lines of having conventional cars fareless, and compartmented cars fared. The advisability of so institutionalizing class differences might be questionable. On the other hand, the well-paid executive who wishes to travel home in total privacy should be able to buy such a privilege. .

4. Ralph Warburton, "Systems Design for Urban Transit," *Journal of the Franklin Institute* 286 (November 1968): 543. Reprinted by permission of the *Journal of the Franklin Institute.*

COMFORT

The comfort and amenities demanded of each type of fixed-route system are almost directly proportional to the trip-times involved. A five minute shuttle-bus or minitrain ride to a nearby transit terminal would not demand the same extent of amenities for the passenger as would a forty minute ride on a medium-speed transit vehicle.

Likewise, this medium-speed trip would not create the amenity demand that a two hour high-speed train trip would. We expect bars, lounges, restrooms, reading lights, enroute meals, and other comforts on our high-speed trains, as we have had past experience with luxury trains. For our low-speed transit devices we need ask for little more than shelter from the weather, temperature control, smooth and silent operation, and reasonable seating accommodations, due to the short travel-times involved.

As we did with the subject of privacy, we must focus here on the medium-speed element of the system, since it is the basic carrier of fixed-route motion. A clue to the comfort standards we would wish of this element is shown in this description of the new BARTD system:

> The seats are roomy and raked at an angle which promises to be comfortable for the relatively long journeys which some of the passengers will have to make from midway down the San Francisco peninsula up to the city itself, across the bay to Oakland and southward to the cities and communities of the East Bay or northward beyond Berkeley. The large windows offer pleasant vistas, the air-conditioning, heating, and ventilation systems are likely to be highly efficient and illumination will be bright, even when trains are in the tunnels. In addition the designers have paid careful attention to the prob-

lem of noise, especially of the cars as they enter and exit from the tunnels.[5]

This should fairly well sum up what we should expect in comfort in this medium-speed category.

ORIENTATION

The concept of orientation, when related to railed transit systems, includes both terminal and vehicle design, as well as all related graphics. Since the passenger in railed transit systems is not actually driving the vehicle and picking his way through the landscape by following signs and landmarks, but is instead riding, he can experience a significant amount of anxiety if he ever has reason to suspect that he has boarded the wrong train, or has missed his station. One of the simplest means of resolving this is to have profuse displays of system maps in each station, with each significant route color-coded. These maps would be repeated inside the transit vehicle, with a display to indicate which route that vehicle is following and which station it is approaching next. Underground stations pose other orientation problems, for no matter how architecturally distinctive they might be, they are still, most often, a world apart from the surface environment above, and offer few orientation clues to the individual not familiar with local station names. A most effective and simple remedy to this has been offered by Peter Chermayeff in Boston's MBTA system: the placement of photomurals in the stations.

> These photomurals are more than decorative. They are graphic reflections of the neighborhood surrounding the station, rec-

5. Ibid., p. 434.

ognizable images of activities and places directly above. The passenger who looks out the window of the train knows from these images that he is passing, for example, under Boston's Public Garden at Arlington Station. The name Arlington takes on a new level of meaning, a new character and identity. The passenger begins to have a sense of place, a new level of awareness of passing through specific areas of his city.[6]

Other design considerations based on orientation needs as handled by Chermayeff include a simplified graphics system; the use of lighting systems as direction-finders; the color scheme—accent colors on significant doors; the shaping and coloring of turnstiles and gates to give a sense of direction; orienting all advertising so it faces the departing passenger only, and does not conflict with the information on the walls facing the arriving passengers; and punching through the roofs of underground stations, constructing skylights "to bring daylight and an awareness of the street to the station platform."[7]

The point is that station design, like vehicle design, is subject to the human needs of those who use the stations, requiring the utmost in sensitive, intelligent design, whether the station is just a boarding-point for a neighborhood bus, or a portion of a huge shopping and office complex, such as Place Bonaventure in Montreal.

CONVENIENCE

Perhaps the most telling measurement of a transport system's convenience is a hard, cold winter rain: any gaps in what

---

6. Peter Chermayeff, "Orientation in the Transit Environment," *Journal of the Franklin Institute* 286 (November 1968): 487. Reprinted by permission of the *Journal of the Franklin Institute*.

7. Ibid.

should be a comprehensive service become brutally apparent. There is nothing like queuing up at an unsheltered bus stop in this kind of weather to make one wish for a true door-to-door transport system. The random-route system can offer this if the doors involved are each located in low-to-medium-density areas, but density levels are growing everywhere . . . and past a point, an area simply cannot provide close-proximity parking. The automobile can serve high-density areas when there is no parking involved, as with taxis, but the limitations of this type of service for handling commuter movement needs become painfully obvious when you try to flag a cab during rush hours on any bad weather day.

What we are really saying when we mention the door-to-door convenience of the automobile is not only that the vehicle is handy to both the departure and destination points, but also that the trip is accomplished without switching vehicles along the way. Unfortunately, at least in most low-density areas, bus stops are not very handy, and most trips cannot be made without switching vehicles. Increasing the number of stops invariably complicates overall routing, and causes increased numbers of necessary transfers. (As mentioned earlier in this text, Washington's Metro planners anticipate 70 percent of their passenger trips will involve at least one bus ride—which would most likely be true with any region-scaled fixed-route commuter movement system.)

Our primary convenience requirement is to be picked up close to our departure point and dropped off close to our destination point. Second, we desire this with a minimum of inconvenience: the least possible exposure to inclement weather; the least possible discomfort and confusion caused by necessary transfers.

Convenience means comprehensiveness: the transport service that provides convenience must be one that provides comprehensive service. Needless to say, our contemporary fixed-route transit systems do not provide this level of service, as they cannot. Should our overall commitment to fixed-route systems be expanded as proposed, however, unfavorable comparisons between fixed-route and random-route convenience factors could be minimized or eliminated if:

(1) Collection points (bus or minitrain stops) are allotted in much greater numbers than now—no point in any residential area should be more than two or three blocks from a pickup point.

(2) Collection points are sheltered, even if only with a sun/rain roof, but preferably with some windbreaking panels (useful for route maps and advertising, incidentally), with a bench for the elderly, the pregnant, and the infirm.

(3) Transfers occur in sheltered areas, so vehicle-to-vehicle exchanges do not have to be pneumonia-inducing experiences.

A comprehensive system layout, combined with appropriate enroute amenities, could easily outstrip the automobile in convenience in any medium-to-high-density area, where door-to-door automobile transport is more accurately door-to-parking lot-to-door transport.

Upgrading fixed-route system standards so that they are equivalent to those of the random-route system, at least in the four areas just discussed, are a necessary step. We must never forget that transportation systems are constructed to serve man, and respect the dignity of man: we cannot accept the cattle-car conditions that typify most of our urban systems.

I have discussed orientation as a design-standard item. However, this encompasses only one facet of the experiential viewpoint of the individual in motion on either system. Unless an individual is confined to a prison cell, or a hospital bed, or the like, he perceives his physical surroundings through motion. We know our surroundings from observations made in sequences of motion-patterns through those surroundings, whether as pedestrians or passengers in vehicles. How much we are able to observe about our surroundings is inversely proportional to the speed at which we move through them: an environment in which we move about as pedestrians, with frequent stops, such as at home or at work, will be known to us in greatest detail; that which we see from a fast moving vehicle is perceived as basic forms and colors.

For example, the automobile passenger who passes through the city of Denver on the main north/south expressway (I-25) is exposed to endless views of factories, warehouse districts, steel scrap yards, etc., throughout the majority of the trip. This expressway rarely allows a glimpse of the gold-domed State Capitol Building or other attractive parts of the city, making one wonder if such parts exist. This, of course, is not a unique invention of Denver: it is the most common of our city-entering experiences. "We tend to slide into cities today as if the encounter were not worthy of great theater," says Lawrence Halprin about this phenomenon.[8]

In the book *Townscape*,[9] Gordon Cullen delineates methods of configuring various English villages and parkways for the desirable sequential experiential aspects presented by these configurations. *The View from the Road* [10] demonstrates the visual-experiential niceties that are theoretically possible for automobile occupants traveling on roadways which are located in places desirable for such purposes, a theme picked up again in *The Freeway in the City*.[11] It is a bit late, in most cases, to

8. Lawrence Halprin, *Freeways* (New York: Reinhold Publishing Corp., 1968).

9. Gordon Cullen, *Townscape* (New York: Reinhold Publishing Corp., 1961).

10. Donald Appleyard, Kevin Lynch, and J. R. Myer, *The View from the Road* (Cambridge, Mass.: M.I.T. Press, 1963).

11. *The Freeway in the City* (Washington, D.C.: U.S. Government Printing Office, 1968).

try to crank this criterion into the random-route system. However, if we contemplate a new fixed-route system, we would be foolish to disregard these design considerations. Any new fixed-route system could be below-grade in same instances, on grade in others, above-grade (elevated) in others, and even passing through structures in yet other cases. Of course, the vertical configuration for the most part would be determined by system-environment compatibility in each instance. However, what the individual experiences as he moves along, under, over, and on the surface is of immense importance: it contributes greatly to the overall quality of life within the physical environment, as so much of that environment is perceived through this motion.

I have experienced an outstanding example of this on the MBTA in Boston. The westbound Boston-Cambridge line is underground at the CBD. As the train moves west toward Cambridge it dramatically pops up out of the tunnel onto the Longfellow Bridge to cross over the Charles River. During this, the passenger is treated to an exciting view of the river, often active with sailboats and racing shells, along with a glimpse of the M.I.T. campus, before the train noses down into the tunnel on the far side. No doubt this visual experience is the accidental blessing of an engineering decision to go over rather than under the river. Yet, if we introduce such visual experiences as design criteria, we are not at the mercy of "accidents." The opportunities for creating similar situations in almost every city are many; it is up to us to take fullest advantage of them.

The designer of a random-route roadway, such as an urban expressway, is handicapped in terms of responsiveness to passenger's experiential viewpoints, or, perhaps more importantly, in terms of the impact of his roadway on right-of-way land-use. This is basically due to the landspace required by a random-route roadway to handle the prevailing traffic loads—it is too wide to be buried in tunnels to any practical extent, and its detrimental effect (primarily noise) on a neighborhood is only magnified when it is elevated. On the other hand, fixed-route systems can be placed in tunnels without passenger capacity loss, and, despite the blighting effects of the old "El" systems (Chicago, Boston, Philadelphia, and New York), can be elevated with a minimal disruption to the landscape—primarily due to the introduction of lightweight vehicles, concrete and/ or welded steel tracks, and electric drive systems, all of which

Figures 7-1, 7-2, 7-3.
Old elevated rail systems are no less blighting than expressways (7-1), but new light-weight systems, more sensitively designed, such as BART (7-2) and the EXPO '67 Minitrain (7-3), make the elevated option valuable in cases where a surface system is incompatible with surface activities, and tunneling is too expensive, or where elevating is desirable for the passenger experience.

allow virtually silent operation. Anyone exposed to the fixed-route system tour-de-force at EXPO '67 will acknowledge that the various elevated systems there were compatible with almost all land-use activities, and, if anything, added a certain amount of visual interest to the environment.

Be that as it may, the transportation planner is faced with a complex set of choices when he must lay out a route between point "A" and point "B," be it a "random" route or a "fixed" route. He must not only face horizontal placement decisions, but vertical placement decisions as well. He must face the reality of interposing his route-line on the fabric of the existing environment. He must also be aware (if he is appropriately sensitive to such things) of the sequential-experience aspects of traveling on this route when it is completed. He must do

this in the face of the installation expenses—as a rule, a route-way (random or fixed) is three times as expensive elevated as when on-grade, ten times as expensive when below-grade.

As mentioned before, the random-route system does not lend itself to much responsiveness to passenger-experience or right-of-way environment conditions, but the fixed-route system does. An example of how this potential can be realized is with the new Seattle fixed-route system. The planning firm of Oka-moto/Liskamm (San Francisco) developed the following chart as a planning tool for that system, which should prove useful for future fixed-route planning.

What we are saying is that we want a transportation system that will allow us the greatest choices possible in the environment. By this, I mean a system that does not prohibit pedestrian-oriented urban spaces; one that does not cut great swaths through neighborhoods (as with destructive expressways); one that offers, as much as possible, door-to-door transport; one that appropriately serves low-density residential areas, yet

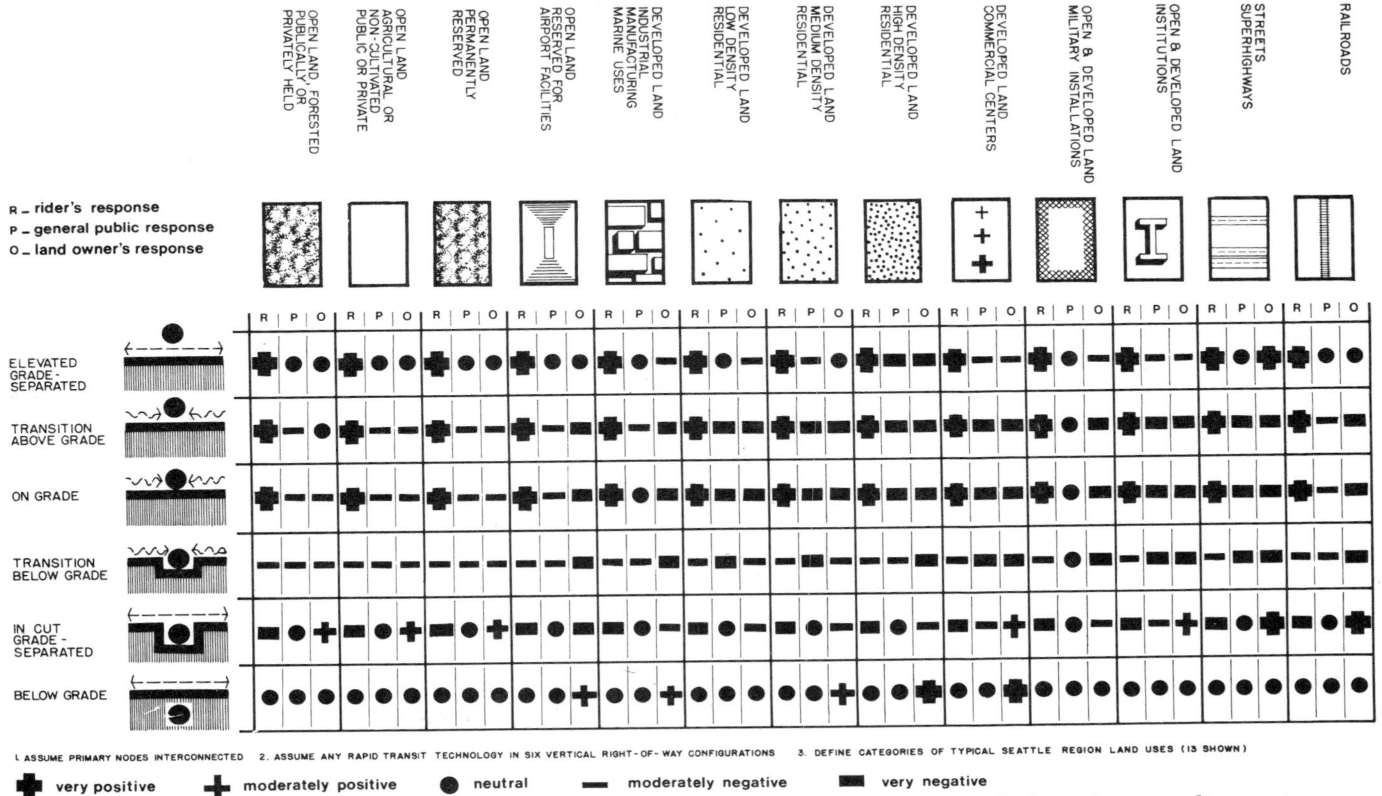

Figure 7-4. An elementary but useful chart for evaluating the environmental effect of various alignments on typical land-use areas. Drawing by Rod Freebairn-Smith for Okamoto/Liskamm, Planners and Architects AIA (Seattle Metropolitan Rapid Transit proposal, 1967–69). Courtesy of the Journal of the Franklin Institute.

does not act as an irresponsive breeder of these developments; one that honors the dignity of man, both as a passenger and an inhabitant of the landscape through which the system is passing. We want efficient service, whether in high- or low-density circumstances, but not at the price of blighting the environment.

Unfortunately, we are not now served properly or adequately, the contemporary service is blighting the environment, and the functional and environmental problems are multiplying. We need to learn how to apply the operational characteristics of the random- and fixed-route systems to the task of organizing a comprehensive and responsible total system.

Eight

TO PLAY THE GAME

ANY SPECULATION on the advantages of such a large-scale proposal as I have outlined is at best only academic if it does not include an analysis of the "hows" involved in establishing the proposal as a reality.

Actually, there are few technological difficulties involved in this proposal. The talent and skills necessary exist today: if we are technologically capable of lunar exploration, we are certainly technologically capable of establishing region-wide, fixed-route transportation systems.

As in most human activities, the factor which most often determines the accomplishment of a major project is not technology, but desire. But aligning the will of the people behind a public transportation scheme is an extremely difficult thing to do. The Montreal Metro system was salable to the public only as a support device for Expo '67. The in-production Washington, D.C. system was finally kicked off after years of negotiations because of the increasing discomfort to the great number of federal employees who must work in an extremely concentrated activity node—a node that simply cannot accommodate many parked automobiles. The Bay Area Rapid Transit Development (BARTD) and the Seattle system are each the

115

product of years of argumentation and political manipulation. On the other hand, Los Angeles residents consistently reject the establishment of such systems.

It is hard to motivate the large middle-class populations of most cities toward the adoption of an expensive system which would seem to provide them with little service, since these people are scattered throughout suburbia, which no existing bus system serves in any comprehensive manner. Railed systems are not usually designed to serve these areas any better, and since both rail and bus systems serve the high-density urban "core" housing areas (usually low-income), they are considered the "poor man's transportation," and therefore do not attract the unqualified support of the automobile-oriented middle-classes.

This resistance, combined with a reluctance to consider any form of change at any time, and a belief that the automobile is eternal, make it difficult for proposals concerning the expansion of public transit services to get a hearing in most communities. Most of our transit systems are thus perpetuated in their present form, and are declared appropriate, when in fact they are not.

The federal government, through the Federal Highway Act, will pay 90 percent of the cost of an urban expressway (the highway people can draw from a "highway trust fund" which contains $4 billion a year, fed by gasoline and tire taxes),[1] the other 10 percent handled locally.

On the other hand, the federal government will only subsidize two-thirds the equipment and facilities costs of rail transit systems, as provided by the Urban Mass Transportation Act of 1964. (The Bay Area Rapid Transit came along too early to profit from this Act: federal assistance totalled $52 million,

---

1. *City Chronicle* (Washington, D.C.: Urban America, Inc., 1969).

only one-twentieth of a net total cost of $1,042 million. Washington's Metro did fall under the Act, with federal assistance totalling $1,147 million, two-thirds of the net total of $1,720 million.[2]) Even so, a subsidy of two-thirds of the costs of a railed transit project does not begin to equal the 90 percent allotted a highway project. Rail systems are considered to be strictly supplementary elements in the transportation scene: their needs are considered only after those of the highways.

Maintaining the status quo is the order of the day. We can anticipate the reception of a proposal that would place the automobile in a secondary commuter movement role by regarding the following interview with James M. Roche, Chairman of General Motors (conducted by *U.S. News & World Report*):[3]

> Question: Mr. Roche, is there any real measure of the role the automobile industry plays in America's economy?
>
> Answer: I think it is perhaps the most important single factor. The automobile industry and related industries involved in maintaining our motorized-transportation system account for one out of every six jobs in the country.
>
> To look beyond the economic impact, we enjoy the highest degree of personal mobility ever achieved by any people in the world. This has been a very important factor in enabling us to accomplish what we have.
>
> Roughly 80 percent of American families own at least one car. There are 88 million motor vehicles registered in the United States—73 million passenger cars and about 15 million trucks—the backbone of our transportation system.
>
> Another measuring stick is the vast quantity of basic materials we use: 61 percent of the rubber consumed in the

2. BARTD and WMATA figures, January 1970 and July 1969, respectively.
3. "Future of the Automobile," *U.S. News & World Report*, February 10, 1969, pp. 64–71. Copyright 1969 U.S. News & World Report, Inc. Reprinted by permission.

U.S., a third of all the glass, 20 percent of the steel and 10 percent of the aluminum—just to mention a few items.

(We are currently in the midst of the construction of an Interstate Highway System, with an authorized total system size of 42,500 miles.)

Question: Will the revenues from highway sources increase enough to pay for the new roads that will be needed—without raising tax rates?

Answer: That will be determined, in part at least, by whatever inflationary pressures may be evident in the economy. The normal growth in the industry will, of course, mean a greater amount of tax income. But if inflation in costs exceeds this growth, there will have to be some more taxes.

Question: When the Interstate Highway System is finished sometime in the mid-1970's, won't that mean a drop in highway building?

Answer: It's likely to, unless the country recognizes the problems and tries to anticipate the growth in vehicle usage, just as we manufacturers have to try to envision the demand for our product.

Question: Are you suggesting that we build more interstate highways beyond the 42,500 miles now authorized?

Answer: If we're going to have the vehicle population that we envision, we're going to have to.

The big problem is moving cars in and out of cities, whether it's interstate travelers or people commuting back and forth in the morning and evening. This is the bottleneck.

(What should be evident to any observer is that this is not simply a question of who should pay. In any case, it is the public who pays. It is more a matter of determining where this money goes, which is another way of saying it is a matter of who represents the Vested Interests Involved, and who is Established. In the United States we have two organizational elements which constitute the power structure of land transportation: the automobile industry (and associated industries) and the state highway departments (backed by the Federal Highway Act). The attitude of these elements toward a proposal that would reduce the random-route system to a minor role in terms of regional urban transportation, and would boost the role of public fixed-route systems, should be obvious.)

Question: What will the automobile population be by 1980?

Answer: Somewhere in the area of 115 million passenger cars, probably 25 million trucks.

Question: Is the time coming when the country will have all the cars it wants or can use?

Answer: We don't think so. There was a saturation point forecast a long time ago—I think in 1927—when we had 21.5 million vehicles. A very prominent economist in the Middle West said that this was as far as the automobile industry was going to go; that the saturation point had been reached; that the purchasing power of the people, combined with the road system, made it impossible for the automobile industry to progress beyond that point.

Question: But isn't there a limit to the number of cars, in terms of roads and parking, in places such as New York City?

Answer: Obviously, we have to find a way to take care of the growing number of cars. We're going to have to find parking facilities, build roads, throughways, freeways—whatever you want to call them—to accommodate this growth. Up to now, we have been fairly successful in doing that.

Question: We were talking earlier about traffic, congestion, city parking and so on. How does the auto industry feel about increasing rapid transit?

Answer: We in General Motors feel—and I think the industry shares this view—that what we need is a combination of private and public transportation. There are areas where a public transportation system can serve more advantageously than an automobile.

On the other hand, there are areas where the reverse is true. We think the city of the future is going to have to have a blend of all systems of transportation. We need the automobiles, we need the buses, we need rail transportation.

There are some cities in the United States that have a very fine system of rail transportation—New York, for example, and the Chicago area.

Question: Isn't the question here what share of public money should go for highways, as against public transportation?

Answer: Yes, but remember that the public money comes from different sources, and I think that the automobile owners and the automobile industry have done a pretty good job of taking care of the expenditures that can be charged against the automobile.

I think the latest estimate is for the year 1966, when there was about 13 billion dollars in taxes paid by the automobile industry and by automobile users—excise taxes, sales taxes, license fees, the gasoline tax and so on—local, state and federal.

Question: Where did that money go?

Answer: Much of it went for new highways and for maintenance of streets and highways.

Question: Are you opposed to using any of this tax money for public transportation?

Answer: Yes—as an industry we are opposed to that.

(Economist John Kenneth Galbraith, in *The New Industrial State,* maintains that any corporation has as its utmost priorities: (1) its continued existence; and (2) its growth.)[4]

4. John Kenneth Galbraith, *The New Industrial State* (New York: New American Library, Inc., Signet Edition, 1967), p. 181.

Question: Is there local resistance to tearing down buildings to build freeways?

Answer: That is one of the problems we are encountering in many cities. One of the answers is decentralization—some industries moving out of cities. One of the important considerations that we have, for example, whenever we undertake a new project is to find a location where we're sure we can provide parking facilities.

Question: But aren't more downtown offices being built all the time, adding to the numbers of commuters?

Answer: That's true in New York, but Manhattan is a special situation. The number of jobs in the downtown Detroit area is holding about stable. One of the problems that we have in Detroit is finding work for people in the inner city. We are now trying to get back some of the business that has left the inner city, and I think this is true in some other areas as well.

It would seem that Mr. Roche is a bit torn between decentralization and "bringing back some of the business that has left the inner city." What he does not seem confused about is that despite any environmental problems, his aim is the continued production and proliferation of automobiles. He is not the villain of this piece—only what he represents. He makes verbal concessions to public transportation systems, but obviously regards such systems as special-use items which do not really threaten his industry. He indicates that the roadway portion of the random-route system is supported to a great extent by user taxes, which is not quite as meaningful as it seems, since the random-route system is so extensive that almost every individual or family in the United States is represented in this user category. Were these same users using a public fixed-route system to the same extent, the equivalent user taxes would be collected in one manner or another. The automobile industry clearly does not want random-route user taxes diverted for fixed-route systems, for obvious reasons.

The random-route industry includes the automobile manufacturers, the petroleum industry, and the highway construction industry, as well as the steel, rubber, glass, and other supply industries. Mr. Roche estimates that one out of every six jobs in the United States belongs in the above category. Placing the basic commuter movements of our metropolitan regions on fixed-route systems could not be considered to be in the best interests of the random-route industry, as the primary use of the automobile is for commuter movements. It would be difficult to predict the actual long term effects on automobile purchasing, but restrictions on automobile movements in key areas, combined with convenient and responsive fixed-route access to those areas, would most probably cause a decline. Whether a realistic threat or not, however, the industry can be counted on for rallying a broad and powerful base of resistance against any proposal for other forms of transportation.

This resistance is reinforced by that of the various state highway departments, whose personnel see their livelihood threatened by any systematic movement that would discourage the continuous production and maintenance of an extensive highway network. These departments are almost autonomous in terms of road construction, and very defensive about their positions. A measure of the resistance of these departments to regional fixed-route systems that would extensively modify the random-route system as we know it might be gleaned from their resistance to a federal proposal that would require that they be responsive to social and environmental needs in their highway building, as reported in *Business Week*.[5] During the

5. "Giving People a Voice on the Highways," *Business Week*, December 14, 1968.

last weeks of the Johnson administration, Transportation Secretary Alan S. Boyd and Federal Highway Administrator Lowell K. Bridwell pushed a proposal that would give the public a louder voice in the road-planning process. It required state highway departments to hold two public hearings on federal-aid projects instead of one—the first before the path of the highway is set, the second before design plans are approved. The proposal also allowed for appeals to the Federal Highway Administrator for individuals dissatisfied with the manner in which the state had met twenty-one basic factors detailed by the Department of Transportation, factors including: residential and neighborhood character and location, conservation, natural and historic landmarks, property values, replacement housing, and displacement of families and businesses. This proposal lined up the "anti" and "pro" highway forces; urban planners, architects, civic groups, conservationists, and home owners, joined by the last administration's Secretary of H.U.D., Robert Weaver, and the Interior Department's Stewart L. Udall, supporting the proposal; and the state highway departments, joined by road construction companies, oil, trucking, and auto trade associations, as well as lobbyists and "state's rights" congressmen opposing the proposal. The position of these two opposing sides can be determined by this representative commentary:[6]

> Wilmington (Del.) architect: "A most important breakthrough in the long battle between good community planning and the refusal by most state highway departments to listen to any recommendations."
>
> Texas Highway Commission: "If the administration persists and the new rule isn't subsequently set aside by Congressional action, the commission says it would favor abandonment of the federal aid program in the state."

6. Ibid.

The state highway departments were logically organized to assure the smooth expansion of the random-route system throughout the state. For this purpose they were endowed with great funds and great authority, including the right to acquire roadway landspace by legal confiscation. Unfortunately, the states unwittingly made these departments the most influential environment-shapers, but did not incorporate into them the checks and balances that such environment-shapers must have if they are to act properly. The departments, after years of power, authority, and virtual autonomy react predictably when belated attempts are made to make them responsible to the social and physical environment they so greatly affect.

I attended a city council meeting in the Texas state capitol (Austin) a few years ago at which a proposed urban expressway was discussed. As the expressway was to be constructed within the city limits, the city was entitled to conduct hearings on the subject. The expressway was proposed to form a faster and larger-than-existing movement-path between the suburbs in north Austin and the CBD. The proposed route was to pass between the large campus of the University of Texas and a large, relatively dense residential area which contains a significant percentage of the student housing for the university. At the hearing, sociologists demonstrated how the expressway would form a highly undesirable barrier between the campus and the housing neighborhood, property owners demonstrated how the expressway would destroy considerable property for residential use, and architects talked about the possibility of preserving the basic pedestrian nature of this area by suppressing the roadway below grade and constructing on-grade pedestrian walkways across it. The representatives of the Texas Highway Department both scoffed and cursed among themselves during the course of this presentation, and, during rebuttal, stated simply that their proposed expressway was the cheapest approach possible and would have the least impact on the taxpayer. The hearing ended with the subject shelved "for study."

In reference to the aforementioned federal proposal for hearings and appeals, New York's Commissioner of Transportation J. Burch McMorran stated: "I'm not upset about two hearings. We've had two, sometimes three. But I do object to the appellate procedure which would take decisions out of our hands and put them into the federal court." A New Hampshire homeowner demonstrated, as did the Austin hearing, why the state departments are not so upset by the hearings part of the proposal: "Here, all too often, public hearings are merely a legal gesture. The public is shown plans all completed and there is not the slightest intention of any change." [7]

What must be understood is that the procedures and attitudes described are not unique to the bureaucratic state highway departments. There is no reason to believe that a fixed-route transit authority would automatically possess virtues that the highway authorities do not display. Replacing a bureaucratic organization dedicated to one form of transportation with one dedicated to another form of transportation is clearly not the total answer. I believe that the fixed-route system has certain characteristics which make it more desirable for regional commuter movement than the random-route system. Also, I contend that the fixed-route system has a greater potential for improving the quality of the physical environment within the Regional Urban Environment at this time than the random-route system. However, when we talk about potential, we are talking about human skills. Any system, within limits,

7. Ibid.

is potentially good or bad, depending to a great extent on how it is handled, as is aptly demonstrated by the miserable quality of most of our older fixed-route transit systems.

An agency dedicated solely to the most efficient method of organizing a fixed-route system is no more desirable than one dedicated solely to the most efficient method of routing expressways. The key to this is the makeup of the agency: the amount of talent and quality and kinds of training those individuals involved possess, and what they consider as their policy goals. We are caught in the dilemma of: "the intellectual preoccupation with efficient means *vs.* the poetic concern for worthwhile ends." [8] Simply enough, the existing transportation agencies are dominated by the engineering professions, which are, if anything, dedicated to "efficient means." Representation of the "poetic concern for worthwhile ends" is so far removed from the seats of power as to be ineffective.

We can see that the established random-route system has solid support from the automotive and related industries, and the state highway departments. Yet, there is another element that would most likely resist a regional changeover from road to rail transportation: the land industry.

Stewart Udall's book, *The Quiet Crisis*,[9] traces the introduction of the concept of land ownership to this continent by the early European settlers, a concept that prevails as an ethic of the free enterprise system today. Every square foot of land in the United States, unless retained by the state or federal governments for parks or reservations or roadway right-of-ways, is "owned" by individuals or corporations or churches (approximately one-third). The buying and selling of property

8. James H. Billington, "A Ferment of Intellectuals," *Life Magazine,* January 10, 1969, p. 96.
9. Stewart Udall, *The Quiet Crisis* (New York: Avon Books, Discus Edition, 1967).

in this country is an immense business, because the owner of property profits or loses from land-use changes that occur on his property. As transportation changes land use, it also effects the real estate market.

The prospects of a region-wide fixed-route system which would determine on a region-wide basis the location of every station-point in the region would not endear itself to most professional land dealers, as it would tend to stabilize the geographical location of land uses in the region, with activities concentrating in activity nodes, and so on, as I have described before. The speculative develop-as-you-can approach of contemporary land dealers would be stymied to a large extent if central planning control of the regional environment decreed that certain areas were to remain undeveloped, and reinforced this planning decision by withholding transportational access from those areas. With the present random-route system, every significant roadway is a potential commercial strip, with possible profits to be made for those who possess the adjacent landspaces. The extensiveness of the random-route system, along with a growing population, with the continuous shifts in land use due to both, keep the land dealers in high cotton. A more stabilized environment, whatever its advantages to the regional population as a whole, would not be to the satisfaction of those who make their livelihoods by profiting from environmental instability. (One dream of some planners in this country is to obtain municipal ownership of large tracts of urban land, thereby establishing land-use controls through deed restrictions on the resale or leasing of this land, as is currently done in Stockholm and other European cities. However, the resistance such public land ownership would meet in this country would exceed that which would oppose the land-use manipulations that the proposed transportation system would create.)

One might gather that the deck is thoroughly stacked against a large-scale road-to-rail commuter movement changeover in this country in the near future, an observation that is not entirely incorrect. Yet, the fixed-route system does retain a few aces. For one thing, every place there is a roadway, the land under that roadway is lost to the tax rolls—a factor that becomes quite significant in dense activity nodes, such as CBDs, where the roadway system uses up to (or more than) 50 percent of the landspace, a reasonable argument for adapting a transportation system that uses far less landspace. Also, the physical crowding in these same areas is defining the limits of the random-route system: fixed-route systems, which move great numbers of people and no automobiles, are becoming mandatory in many areas of the United States. Also, the concern for the total environment, and the desire to control the environment with man's long-term needs in mind is no passing fancy. A clue to the growing concern about transportation/environment relationships is demonstrated in the pioneering establishment in Baltimore of an integrated team of planners, sociologists, architects, and highway engineers involved in urban expressway planning in the Baltimore area, applying the Urban Design Team approach pushed by the Bureau of Public Roads through the inspired guidance of Federal Highway Administrator Lowell K. Bridwell. This experiment is not passing unnoticed by concerned professionals elsewhere.

There can be no question that more and more fixed-route systems will appear on the scene. The question instead is whether they will appear in a form that comprehensively serves and benefits the total environment, or in a form that contributes to the overall chaos that is condemning our environment at this time.

To effect proper total control over the physical environment in the United States, we will probably have to alter our basic governmental structures in this area. The existing Regional Urban Environment "Megalopolis," extending from Washington, D.C., to Boston, encompasses parts of ten states, each with its own governmental agencies. The United States is slow to grasp the concept of regional governments, as instigated in England and several European countries. The Regional Urban Environment begs for regional control, but it is not yet here. The federal government takes that part of regional control that can be classified as "interstate commerce," such as the Interstate Highway System—yet, the federal government is not the proper administrative body for the Region, any more than the multitudes of state, county, and city governments. The establishment of regional governments that correspond to the various Regional Urban Environments will not be quick in coming (although they most probably will come some day), as their arrival would mean the subjugation, or even dissolution, of the states as we know them, within these regions. The resistance to this type of thinking is obvious; yet, interestingly enough, the Center for the Study of Democratic Institutions has come to a similar conclusion: they opt for a set of twelve regions, abolishing all the states.[10] While this particular proposal is not structured to correspond with the existing and developing Regional Urban Environments, there is no reason why it couldn't be.

We are not totally inexperienced with regional governments. An advocate of them, Carl Feiss (planning consultant), describes our most successful experiment with them—the Tennessee Valley Authority:

> TVA makes geography the basis of human planning and contrivance; it makes use of the region, which is the middle choice between the extremes of federal centralization and a

10. *Time* January 24, 1969, p. 54.

limited local jurisdiction. The regional device helps to check the march toward federal centralization and at the same time avoids the anarchy that sometimes results when local authorities try to solve piecemeal problems that transcend local boundaries.

The TVA grew slowly from the Congressional franchise of Hales Bar in 1905 until the Tennessee Valley Authority Act of 1933. Since then its program has become known, admired, and imitated throughout the world, except in the United States. We seem to be scared of our own success . . . it may well be that the planners of the country do not know the TVA, its accomplishments, and its potential as an example of a new order in national affairs. In any case, I am recommending here and now that the TVA program is the one and only sound basis on which to build the new American Dream and that its experience and vitality be drawn upon for the solution to the resource and resettlement problems that face the nation. I would blanket the country with such mechanisms. I would prepare plans within the selected areas, manage and implement them as has the TVA; and I would involve every level of government and private enterprise as has TVA.

This is not just a pat solution. At the moment no one in politics would dare make such a suggestion. I urge, however, that we as planners look at the record, look at our history, take stock, and propose action. I challenge one and all to come up with a better solution.[11]

Since I contend that transportation is one of the greatest single environmental form-determinants, and that total control over transportation means, to a large extent, control over the environment, it follows that the establishment of regional transportation authorities is essential. Establishing such authorities seems a monumental task on one hand, but less a task than the establishment of regional governments, on the other.

11. Carl Feiss, *Environment and Change*, pp. 235–36.

The regional transportation authority is a must in any case, whether the commuter road-to-rail proposal described in the book be augmented or not. Interdependencies and interrelationships of regional motion patterns cry for overall coordination and planning at this time, and the situation becomes more complex as time goes on. Of course, if this authority were merely a larger version of our contemporary state counterparts, we would be but little better off. The composition of talents and personalities in the regional transportation authority would be all-important. If regional transportation is to be both efficient and man/society/environment oriented, it must be administered by professionals from areas of efficiency, competence, and aesthetics. This transportation authority would also have to conduct its affairs openly: if it is to work in a responsible, professional manner, it will welcome hearings and public examinations of its policies; and would support a just redress clause, recognizing this as a method of protecting the individual for whom that authority is ultimately constructed to serve.

Some of the aspects involved in establishing a Regional Transportation Authority can be found in the experiences of consultants with the (1) Atlanta, (2) San Francisco, and (3) Seattle fixed-route projects.

(1) Leon Eplan, director of the Corridor Impact Study for the Metropolitan Atlanta Rapid Transit Authority (MARTA), observes:

> There appear to be two important reasons for the primitive state-of-the-art in transportation planning. One has to do with a definition of the role of transportation, and the other with the muddled responsibility of making vital and difficult choices regarding the community.
>
> The role transportation will play has been far too narrowly drawn. Overriding all other considerations in the evaluation

of a system is its operation within a system of like facilities: the function of a road within a system of roads, that of an airport within a system of airports. While such an evaluation needs to be made of every transportation system, the overemphasis on this narrow systems approach has dwarfed in importance other considerations, producing models to test and computers to feed, but little sensitivity to the community which supposedly is to be served. The original cost of constructing a transportation facility, for example, is still the central basis for determining a route location, despite the existence of many other immediate and delayed costs: the damage to a neighborhood, the dislocation of businesses, the added burden of recovering from the placement of a facility in a built-up area. Likewise, the analysis of the benefits of a facility is almost totally restricted to users of the systems—the travelling public. This remains the method of evaluation even though the opportunities of creating an exciting facility are largely excluded from the benefit equations, as are the questionable (or negative) benefits to the nontravelling public.

What is responsible for this narrow definition? In most cases involving highways, the guilt has rested on the engineer. And for good reason; for his training in the planning of urban expressways is limited, and his practices reveal this lack of skill. The placing of the blame entirely on the highway engineer, however, is unfortunate because it relieves the decision-makers of their responsibility for understanding what the highway will do to, or can do for, the community. The engineer is normally doing what he is hired to do, that is, to build highways. Unfortunately, he is often required to do highway planning when local communities have abdicated the responsibility. It is here that the definition of what the road (or airport or rapid train) should and can do, narrows. Perhaps not in every case is the local leadership at fault, but in many cases where conflicts arise, the mayor and council, the planner and his commission, and other local leadership groups in and out of government have failed to provide the engineer with a plan based on a local commitment to use the transportation system to carry out their idea of the good community. The ability of a highway to define and rebuild neighborhoods, to revitalize business districts, to provide parks, to overcome the isolation of the poor, and other goals, is lost; and the ability of the road to move cars is all that remains.

Besides this narrow definition of what a transportation system is all about, there is a second problem in relating this system to the metropolitan area. This is in the division of responsibility for metropolitan affairs. The National Highway Act of 1962, which required comprehensive, coordinated and continuous highway planning in metropolitan areas, finally overcame the unrelated activities in these urban areas. But there is still little relationship between transportation systems and other systems, policies, and facility planning. Schools, airports, poverty programs, utilities, cultural facilities, zoning practices (not to mention the private activities) all create plans and perform services of great importance, each well-devised and expensive. Unfortunately, few show any relationship to each other, despite the fact that each affects the other's plans.

Each of these independent activities, furthermore, is responsible only for its own affairs. The highway people are not trying to solve school problems; at best, they try not to worsen them. In fact, there is nothing in the mission of the transportation planner to help provide parks, to preserve older neighborhoods, to beautify the urban environment, or to serve a public arena, especially when the cost of achieving these aims may be higher than not achieving them, and the patronage might even be lower. Rapid transit in Atlanta, for example, may not serve the new stadium despite the fact that, when in use, this sports center has the highest patronage of any single facility in the metropolitan area—so large that three interstate highways become practically inoperative when a game is being played. Furthermore, the stadium lost a half million dollars last year, a deficit that had to be repaid by the taxpayers. Rapid transit could serve this arena, reduce its deficits, unclog its highways, and keep it from spending vast sums for additional parking. But the rapid transit authority has its own operation to justify, and though the same taxpayers pay the bills, the authority feels that it should not pay for the privilege of possibly reducing the huge losses being borne by other facilities, especially when, on a patronage basis, a stadium station cannot be justified. This sort of divided responsibility over urban conditions sharply reduces the chances that we can ever resolve our urban problems.[12]

(2) Consultants Maule and Burchard of the San Francisco BARTD system have these observations:

A system like BARTD will inevitably bring enormous economic advantages and perhaps diseconomies to a few. But neither is planned. The narrowness of BARTD's powers coupled with the lack of real planning preparedness in any of the communities in which BARTD is being built to serve, guarantees this. Given their charter, BARTD people may even have exceeded their authority in trying for so many neighborhood conversations as they did. But the major ingredient was missing, the power of the transport district to make its own investments which might have then helped to subsidize the transportation itself; or at least to be able to take enough land in the neighborhood of all stations, except the most central ones, to ensure the kind of orderly development whereby the public interest as well as the private might have been fostered. Such powers could have been adequately guarded against abuse, as they presumably have been in Montreal. They would have materially increased the flexibility and amenity of station design and promoted a much better total system. Their absence and the narrowness with which the available powers have been construed have not only forfeited some non-recurrent communal opportunities but in a few cases

---

12. Leon S. Eplan, "The Impact of Rapid Transit on Atlanta," *Journal of the Franklin Institute* 286 (November 1968): 388–89. Reprinted by permission of the *Journal of the Franklin Institute*.

have actually produced minor disasters on sites where recalcitrant adjacent property owners have proved impossible to negotiate with. Fortunately, there are not many of these. But it is a pity that wider powers were not given which could have led to major local improvements so that the major fruits would not fall, often by sheer accident, to small and frequently not very civic-minded entrepreneurs from morticians to minor-league supermarket owners.

The final point we would make is that the early history points up an example of another important common problem in the design of the complex systems where many skills are needed and where no one should be dictatorially dominant even if his field accounts for a large percentage of the work. This issue should not be reduced to the simple worn-out question as to who ought to be on top, with the corollary that architects are improvident and unrealistic (as many, alas, are) and that engineers are insensitive (as many, alas, are). No Utopian, new education will, we think, correct this among the various specialists. The real problem in any very large venture is not the profession of the skipper but his quality. Big-name architects simply create other difficulties if they are dominant. Most of the time engineers will probably have the leadership. It is not the fault of most of them if they feel architecture and landscaping are a sort of nice cosmetic which can be applied if there is enough time and money in the end. Little of their education or even their subsequent experience causes them to realize that the landscaping and the architecture will be better if all the principals participate in the very first decisions when conditions are being set. Not all early engineering decisions have the stamp of inevitability. Debate usually exists even within the limits of engineering criteria, and very often in the end no measurable set of facts can point to one decision as being uniquely rational. In such a situation (for all but the most primitive systems) it is possible that an architectural consideration, if heard, might point to a different engineering conclusion. We mean here more, of course, than this because,

though a few present architects talk a fast sociological or an-
thropological game, they are, in fact, no better informed about
these, also important factors, than the engineers. So the team
needs to be a little larger than the one we have been discussing, especially in the early decision making.

BARTD has suffered some from too many preconditions set
by engineering, a priority which considered from the point of
view of engineering alone may have been perfectly sound. At
the top in engineering organizations, theoretical and philosophi-
cal talk can sometimes be engaged. On the front lines, decisions are likely to be taken as immutable and the project sped
on its way in the spirit of Admiral Farragut. Thus when it
appears that a better architectural solution might have been
possible we were, for a time, told that it was too late, that it
would cost too much in time and money to change. This is an
annoying argument but by the time it is made it may, in fact,
be true. The point is, of course, that it should never have been
possible to make it. The establishment of genuine dialogue
between all the designing and planning teams at the very
beginning of decision making and the consistent follow-up to
be sure the dialogue continues and that no eager beaver is to
be allowed to swim against its tide, this is the only way
around a great difficulty which is not caused because any par-
ticipant is intentionally evil or stupid. And if this can become
a way of life then it will not matter so much whether King
Log or King Stork seems to wear the crown.[13]

(3) In contrast to the dissatisfaction expressed by Maule
and Burchard over the way BARTD was handled, Rai Okamoto, consultant on the Seattle Rapid Transit Study, has this
observation:

The Seattle work as a pioneer venture in the design team ap-

13. Tallie B. Maule and John E. Burchard, "Design Procedures for the Bay
Area," *Journal of the Franklin Institute* 286 (November 1968): 434–36, 442.
Reprinted by permission of the *Journal of the Franklin Institute*.

proach was given strong leadership and participation by the city government, notably by Mayor J. D. Bramen and his staff. The members of the design team began work together, far in advance of implementation. No previous transit-planning process had undertaken such a full interdisciplinary approach with a vital social-political framework. Transit's causal relation to the city's social, economic, and physical behavior was made part of the design process for the first time. This method sought maximum congruence between both transit and broader community goals and requirements. Transit was viewed as a servant system, an attitude that placed soft-wear criteria on a par with the hard.[14]

Ralph Warburton, a Special Secretary to the Secretary of H.U.D., has outlined what he calls Integral Design, an approach for planning fixed-route systems:

> There are six basic physical planning segments of Integral Design: General Planning, Intensive Planning, Urban Design, Station Design, Right-of-Way Design, and Vehicle Design.
> General Planning is concerned with broad metropolitan and city data trends, and alternative strategies which can influence the location of and use within the transit corridor. Intensive Planning for the one- or two-mile-wide corridor consists of more detailed studies including those for rehabilitation and zoning. Urban Design, for an area comprising at least the $\frac{1}{6}$ to $\frac{1}{4}$ mile pedestrian radius around the station, develops the specific three dimensional potential of the environment. (This scale of design should also be applied along the Right-of-Way where the line is elevated.) Right-of-Way Design is concerned with the specific alignment and functioning of the vehicle supporting structure, and Vehicle Design with the passenger carrier configuration and operation.

14. Rai Okamoto, "Urban Design Determinants in Seattle and New York," *Journal of the Franklin Institute* 286 (November 1968): 402. Reprinted by permission of the *Journal of the Franklin Institute.*

Appropriate attention to each of these activities requires the predominance of certain types of professional experiences.

Activity	Urban Planner	Architect, Landscape Architect	Engineer	Industrial Designer
General Planning	X			
Intensive Planning	X			
Urban Design	X	X		
Station Design		X	X	
R.O.W. Design		X	X	
Vehicle Design			X	X

These basic activities are all relevant, to some degree, in every task phase of development. These tasks include the range from initial feasibility studies to the construction of the system. The capability of each design activity to make inputs and react to feedback should be preserved through organization and funding during every stage of transportation development. Thus the process can integrate development activities, professional skills, and task phases into a degree of continuity not yet achieved.

Successful design for transit depends on the professions as well as the metropolitan client. Architects, landscape architects, and urban planners should be given further responsibilities for transit development. Public officials should be aware, continuously, of the role good design can play. There is much room for experimentation here; for new ideas, for new means of effective cooperation. It is important that all persons who desire a better urban environment translate that concern into Integral Design and, in turn, design the concept into coordinated action.[15]

The establishment and composition of transportation author-

15. Ralph Warburton, "Systems Design for Urban Transit," *Journal of the Franklin Institute* 286 (November 1968): 551–52.

ities on a scale adequate to handle all transportation situations within a region is no simple matter. While the establishment of regional governments might be beyond our grasp at this time, the establishment of regional transportation authorities would be a step in bringing that about. This is because the transportation authority could not function without creating a regional planning agency: the transportation authority would have to be the functional tool of the planning agency. We cannot ever again allow our transportation activities the autonomy they enjoy today, or any independency from our planning activities.

To call then for a regional transportation authority is to call for a regional planning agency, which is ultimately to call for a regional government, which would be the only appropriate agency for granting the powers needed by the former two agencies. It is my opinion that this is ultimately the only realistic approach toward handling our uncontrolled regions. I am concerned that we seem incapable of making such organizational changes on a rapid enough basis to prevent a significant amount of environmental disorder and destruction in the meantime.

Establishing these agencies is no guarantee of a rosy future for the region, yet, this would grant potential developments that are almost impossible to achieve with our multitudinous, noninterrelated governmental agencies that presently struggle with regional problems on a fragmented basis.

The most important factor in establishing regional agencies, as far as this topic is concerned, is the complete and enforced subordination of the regional transportation authority to the regional planning agency: this can never be reversed. A regional fixed-route system, with supplementary random-route systems, demands handling on two levels: operational and planning. The actual administration and operation of such a total system, including continuous expansions and modifications, would demand the range and scope of talents (if not more) that are presently involved in our contemporary random-route system. However, the environmental implications of such a system could not be left to the discretion of those technicians who would construct the system (as we now do with the majority of our expressways, with often disastrous results). However, it would be awkward (and probably totally unworkable) to load up the transportation authority with those talents involved in the many sociological and planning skills needed to give the authority proper guidance: to function properly, the transportation authority would have to be the functional tool of a regional planning agency, which would harbor the appropriate skills and talents, and could integrate all regional environmental situations with the most desirable regional movement activities.

To call for such centralized control over the region is to call for another large bureaucracy to direct our affairs, an inescapable solution, I feel, despite our reluctance to accept such creations willingly. The fact that such a regional government would probably involve no greater number of warm bodies than is invested in the many small governments in the regions today would assuage few of the hard-line objectors to big government of any form. Yet, the choice as I see it is that of rational control of our Regional Urban Environments, which adds up to regional governments, or eventual environmental chaos in the regions, which can be the only result of our present transportation and land-use practices. Relinquishing traditional state, county, and city powers to regional governments would not come easily: it may be instructive to note that many of our traditional institutions are facing challenges from many fronts at this time due to their inappropriateness or incompatibility with planning for a better future.

Finally, these observations:

(1) Our present methods of handling transportation/land-use relationships is unsuitable. We are failing to recognize regions actively and to treat them appropriately. When we do build urban fixed-route systems we fail to link them properly with significant activity nodes in the environment. We seem to be willing to let our random-route system spread wasteful and inappropriate land developments far beyond any vestige of control. We seem to be willing to allow the destruction of every open piece of urban land, and a considerable amount of our rural land, for the sake of preserving the institution of the automobile. We seem willing to wait for our random-route system to break down in some unyielding, dramatic manner, such as having a traffic jam lock a major city into a standstill for an intolerable amount of time, before we face the fact that the random-route system is not our only transportation choice.

(2) The need for fixed-route transportation systems is becoming more and more evident as we go on:

> In the United States at present, the rapid transit vehicles operate 1,300 miles of route over 400 miles of right-of-way, and roughly half the latter mileage is outside of New York City. Five metropolitan areas now have grade separated transit, and some forty or more are in some phase of serious discussion with regard to developing their own systems. In half of these, significant actions are underway. Given the projections, it is very likely that we will double our national transit mileage by 1985.[16]

While this seemingly contradicts the statement that we are not turning to fixed-route systems willingly, we must realize that most of these systems are proposed in belated recognition of the approaching limits to the workability of the random-

16. Ibid., p. 543.

route system in those specific high-density areas . . . and that in those areas that do not possess existing fixed-route systems, the concept of installing them must be sold against monumental resistance. While these systems are generally welcomed by the environment-related professions, the public is most commonly unconvinced.

Yet, in any case, these systems are coming, as conditions force their introduction. The task, then, is to assure that the establishment of these systems is conducted in a manner responsive to the needs of man's environment, and to the needs of the individual.

(3) I believe that in the Regional Urban Environment, where both fixed-route and random-route transportation systems exist, the fixed-route systems must dominate commuter movements. This is for the simple reason that the configuration of the fixed-route system, and thus its environmental effects, can be controlled on a vastly easier basis than the random-route system. The random-route system, with its inescapable characteristics of land development and land-use alteration, cannot be allowed to continue to exist in its present form, as it cannot be made responsive to environmental and human needs due to its sheer size. It is possible to control the random-route system only if it is constrained to limited sizes and only applied in specific circumstances.

(4) If fixed-route systems are to become the dominant commuter movement element in the region, they must be comprehensive in scope. This means, simply enough, that they must touch base with every significant activity node in the region, which means that they will have to provide service that ranges from low-density housing collection systems to high-speed transport between major nodes in the region. No existing or proposed systems yet offer this level of comprehensiveness, yet they are forming the groundwork (either adequately or poorly) for future regional systems.

(5) One of five criteria considered to be appropriate for evaluating an activity as being "professional" is as follows: "the use of technical means as just that and not as ends, recognizing that people are the ends means are designed to serve." [17] Transportation technology of any type represents technical means, not only for the movement of people and goods about the environment, but also for shaping our use of that environment. When we concentrate on the movement aspects, the environmental aspects suffer, and, no doubt, the converse is true also. In order to handle both aspects in a "professional" manner, it is our responsibility to recognize that transportation is a technological tool, and it is our responsibility to know just how this tool works, and to use it in the manner that best benefits man.

Figure 8-1.
Photo by author.

17. William R. Ewald, Jr., *Environment and Change* (Bloomington: University of Indiana Press, 1968), p. xi.

INDEX